LEAVING
Loneliness
BEHIND

"*Leaving Loneliness Behind* is the book you've been looking for. Regina Boyd does an incredible job of taking abstract ideas and turning them into something you can touch, something you can do, and something you can then share with the world. Her use of the emotional roadmap is so insightful, really leading the reader to the ultimate destination: healing and wholeness. I challenge every reader to turn these pages with an open heart. This book is going to change your life."

Rachel Bulman
Contributor to Word on Fire Catholic Ministries

"With honesty and insight, this introduction into the loneliness in every human heart and our desire for connection validates daily experiences and sheds light on pathways forward. Addressing trust and betrayal, relationships and communication, healing and growth—all through the lens of our Catholic faith—Boyd's conversational style and experience will make you feel accompanied."

Sr. Bethany Madonna, SV
Vocations director for the Sisters of Life

"We all yearn for deeper connection and intimacy. Yet our wounds and self-centeredness often become barriers, keeping us isolated. This book (and workbook) based on Regina Boyd's experience as a Catholic therapist is filled with practical wisdom. I highly recommend it. Put her words into practice and your relationships will flourish."

Bob Schuchts
Author of *Be Healed*

"In *Leaving Loneliness Behind*, Boyd offers a sincere path toward connection and communion that does not shy away from difficult realities. She draws not only from her clinical expertise but also is generous in offering the fruit of her own journey and prayer to bring together this work, which is a gift to the Church, especially in our time."

Sr. Josephine Garrett, CSFN
Licensed counselor

LEAVING

Loneliness

BEHIND

5 Keys to Experiencing
God's Love and Building
Healthy Connections
with Others

REGINA BOYD

Founded in 1865, Ave Maria Press is a ministry of the United States Province of Holy Cross.

www.avemariapress.com

Paperback: ISBN-13 978-1-64680-204-3

E-book: ISBN-13 978-1-64680-205-0

Cover image © GettyImages.com.

Cover and text design by Christopher D. Tobin.

Printed and bound in the United States of America.

Library of Congress Cataloging-in-Publication Data is available.

Contents

Introduction

During my years caring for patients, the most
common condition I saw was not heart disease
or diabetes; it was loneliness.
—Vivek Murthy,
Surgeon General of the United States

Natalie is a woman in her early thirties who came to me
for counseling. Prior to meeting me, Natalie appeared to
have it all together. She had a large social circle, and she
was moving fast toward becoming a tenured professor.
She was very close with her sister, whom she considered
her best friend, and her sister's children. She was the cool-
est aunt on the block. She lived the ideal young adult
life: traveling, socializing, vibrant faith life, dating, and
increased responsibilities at work.

But Natalie didn't come to see me to tell me how
perfect her life was. Something had been bothering her,
but it was difficult for Natalie to put a finger on it. Then,
shortly before she came to see me, Natalie's boyfriend
of three years ended their relationship. Suddenly single,
she realized she was lonely. But the loneliness was not
due to the breakup. Natalie realized that she had been
feeling lonely for several years. She had felt lonely for

so long that it was difficult to recall when she hadn't felt lonely.

As she shared more with me, she admitted that she had used the external factors in life—friendships, dating, and work—to distract her from the nagging loneliness. The end of her long-term relationship had just made things bad enough for her to pay attention. She realized she was a worried, anxious, and insecure person. She worried about people judging her for not being married at this point in her life and that others would assume something was wrong with her. She felt like an imposter at work and was afraid that her colleagues recognized her as a fraud when she was promoted. Though she was surrounded by so many people who cared about her and she appeared to have a fulfilling life, she felt detached, misunderstood by others, and alone. "I don't get it," Natalie expressed during our first session. "People have it so much worse than I do. I feel so silly complaining about this. Something just doesn't feel right. I just feel off . . . and really lonely."

What Natalie didn't realize was that she wanted more out of all her relationships, she just didn't know what. Natalie knew how to make friends, how to be social, and how to find a boyfriend, but she didn't know how rich, deep, meaningful, and interpersonal those relationships could be. Friendship and dating had simply never been that way for her. My job was to help her see what she was missing.

Made for Relationships

You were made to taste and see the best of everything God has to offer. One of the remarkable things about God's goodness is that it is experienced primarily in relationships. If you think about the most powerfully positive emotional experiences of your life, how many of them have occurred in the presence of other people? How many with those you love and call friends? There's a good chance that nearly all of them were so. This should come as no surprise to us because relationships are fundamental to human existence. From the moment we are born, we need relationships. Children who grow up surrounded by love thrive in a variety of ways, while children who experience a severe lack of love languish; some even die if the neglect is severe enough. From the moment we are conceived, we are made for relationships and nearly every facet of our lives confirms this reality.

God made us for relationships because he made us like himself. Our God is trinitarian and exists eternally in relationship. We, uniquely in all of creation, reflect this reality in our being. Our whole self—our physicality and our emotional interior life—confirm this. Our experiences of love, intimacy, and longing for closeness confirm this. We are made to love and to be loved. The greatest commandment confirms this. When Jesus was asked by a student of the law to condense the moral life into one commandment, Jesus told us to love God above all things and to love our neighbor as ourselves (Mt 22:36–40). You were made to experience the best of everything God has to offer and you will do this primarily in and through relationships.

Gaudium et Spes highlights the type of relationships we are made for: "This likeness reveals that man, who is the only creature on earth which God willed for itself, cannot fully find himself except through a sincere gift of himself" (sec. 24). This points us back to the words of Jesus in Luke 17:33: "Whoever seeks to preserve his life will lose it, but whoever loses it will save it." The mystery and paradox of our faith is that relationships allow us to experience the fullness of life and self-sacrificing love for the other. Part of the reason Natalie was unsatisfied with her relationships is that those relationships rarely required her to be self-sacrificial. Because she never risked much, she never gained much.

Pope St. John Paul II in his theology of the body refers to this mystery of human love as the spousal meaning of the body. Now, don't worry too much about the term *spousal* here, as Pope St. John Paul II isn't saying that only married couples can love this way. He explains that in marriage, spouses make the mystery of God's love visible in their complete gift of self to each other, in not only the unitive sexual act but also every sincere act of love they make for each other. In other words, the human body reveals the reality that we are made for intimate, self-sacrificial relationships.

This reality follows the pattern of love set out for us by Jesus, who as our bridegroom makes a perfect and perpetual gift of himself on the Cross and in the Eucharist. When we reciprocate that gift, we experience the greatest mystery of all in the love of the Trinity. Just as the heights of human experience occur in relationships, so too does our experience of the divine exist only in a deeply intimate relationship. Relationships with God and neighbor are the key to understanding, experiencing, and participating in the greatest goods possible.

But our lived reality is far from this idyllic vision of perfect relationships with our family, friends, and neighbors. Loneliness has been the sole companion for all of us at some point, and for many of us all the time. Loneliness makes us doubt God's promise, doubt our friends and family, and doubt that we are worthy of being loved at all. It tells us that no one understands us or cares about us. It lies to us and tells us that the people we love would rather not be around us and that they only tolerate us out of pity. Loneliness even tells us that God doesn't really love us, doesn't want to give us himself, and is somehow holding happiness back from us. Loneliness tells us that we are lonely and that we are better off that way, and so it becomes a self-fulfilling prophecy.

I want to help. God gives all of us certain charisms or missions in life. One of mine is to end loneliness. One of my goals in life is to help people establish meaningful relationships by learning how to build and develop emotional intimacy. This is what we seek in relationships. This is what we experience when we live in communion with God and neighbor, entering into the mystery of trinitarian life where we surrender everything and so participate in God's infinite love.

Christianity is not a coping mechanism. If you have a crucifix near you, I invite you to look at it now. If not, try to picture one in your mind. Our God didn't take on human suffering and die on a cross for us to mope through life for eighty years, waiting for eternity to be happy. He came that we might have life and have it abundantly (Jn 10:10). As scripture and saints help us to see and the doctrine of the Incarnation teaches us, Jesus came to redeem everything about being human, including our relationships. If you have ever encountered God in a beautiful moment of prayer, burned with zeal for him in the early stages of your conversion, or tingled with joy in a moment of deep connection with a friend or loved one, then you already know what I am talking about. Those experiences aren't fool's gold. That is the fruit of the emotional intimacy that I am talking about.

This is the adventure God has in store for you when he invites you to follow him, experience life-giving relationships, and live as his heroic witness in the world. He wants your relationships with him and others to be experiences and icons of his love. Ultimately he invites you to share his inner life and know what it is like to love like him.

What Is Emotional Intimacy?

Let's start with a definition of emotional intimacy.

> Emotional intimacy: A relationship quality that allows another to peer into the depths of your heart and soul. It is allowing yourself to share more deeply by expressing feelings, vulnerability, and trust, verbally and by actions. It is an invitation to another to journey alongside you in the beautiful complexity of life and to grow in mutual affection.

Emotional intimacy permeates everything in a relationship and acts as one of the fundamental building blocks for authentic connection. It is the antidote to loneliness. It mediates how close you feel to others and makes everything you do together more enjoyable. If you consider the many relationships you have, it's likely that you enjoy a great deal of emotional intimacy with the people you love and who love you the most. I'd be willing to bet that you don't feel lonely when you are with those people.

Emotional intimacy is what makes relationships meaningful, rich, rewarding, and worthwhile. It is the difference between a relationship that has all the external markers of success but none of the internal harmony, satisfaction, and joy that human beings yearn for. If you've ever known a couple who looked like they had the perfect marriage on the outside but ended up on the rocks, it is likely they lacked emotional intimacy. When emotional intimacy wanes, people become lonely. Lonely people do surprising things, and this is frequently the cause of one or both members of the couple seeking companionship in other people, hobbies, or material goods. Sometimes it is an affair, but it just as frequently looks like a husband spending too much time with his friends, watching sports; a wife giving priority to her girlfriends or close relatives; or an individual engaging in addictive, risky, and destructive behaviors.

Life without deep emotional intimacy can be very lonely. Life with emotional intimacy is fulfilling and draws us into our ultimate calling of communion.

There are five major components to emotional intimacy: (1) connection, (2) trust and vulnerability, (3) communicating during conflict, (4) healing, and (5) self-gift. To have profound closeness in your relationships, all five are necessary. I'll introduce these briefly, but you will have an opportunity to dive deeper as each component will be explored at length in its own chapter.

Connection

Ever have that moment when you just "click" with someone? It doesn't take a lot of effort but somehow you both are on the same page and have a mutual level of understanding that you are compatible and enjoy your time together. That's connection, and it comes from having a sense of closeness and belonging. It means that you and the people you are in relationship with are in the right place, in the right way. We are created for connection and can't live without it.

Trust and Vulnerability

Trust and vulnerability are prerequisites to emotional intimacy. They act as the twin gatekeepers of the other components. A sense of trust and safety is necessary to be vulnerable. Without vulnerability, intimacy simply can't happen. If we aren't willing to risk being hurt, we won't try to connect, we communicate inauthentically, we fear the steps required for healing, and self-gift seems far too risky.

Communicating during Conflict

We all have something to say, and we all desire to be heard. Yet how can something that seems so essential to human activity and society be so difficult at times? As commonplace as communication is, great communicators are in short supply! Communication is what allows us to share ourselves vulnerably and intimately with others and, more importantly, receive without judgment the self-communication of another.

Healing

We've all experienced hurt in our past and it colors how we view our current relationships. Ever wonder why a neutral word or phrase can set you off, or why someone's quirky habit might make you feel very uncomfortable? These can be signs that we have been hurt by someone or something in our past and we can't interpret people neutrally or with charity. Healing these past wounds is often a necessary step that allows us to experience deeper intimacy and a new sense of freedom.

Self-Gift

The paradox that "man . . . cannot fully find himself except through a sincere gift of himself"(*Gaudium et Spes* 24) is the ultimate answer to our pangs of loneliness. The daily interactions with those around us are mini invitations and opportunities to combat loneliness and live out our call to communion with others. All the other keys to emotional intimacy increase our ability to be a gift.

Keep in mind that these five components don't exist in isolation. They overlap with and condition one another. The closeness that you need to feel, a sense of connection, really isn't possible without communication, and sometimes healing is necessary before we know how to make a gift of ourselves to others. While we will discuss them separately, in real life it's not so easy to keep them apart.

Into the Depths

When I talk with my clients, I like to use the analogy of exploring a cave. One of my best friends is a US Air Force wife, and near one of her many stops around the country was an intricate underground cave system. This was novel to me as I've spent almost my entire life in Florida and such geological features are rare and usually underwater. Brave cave divers might venture down there, but that's not for me! But on one of my trips to visit my friend, she took my husband and me to the cave.

Tourists like us were only allowed to go down with the help of a tour guide. We were lucky to have a great guide who seemed to know the cave inside and out. Still, there were plenty of places that were uncomfortable. Some were dark, some were damp, some were cramped, and some were all three. Even with our guide, it was uncomfortable to be down there. At one point, she turned out the lights and it was true pitch black. I had never been so immersed in darkness in my life. Even though I knew my friends were near, I still felt a little scared.

The heart can be like that. It can be uncomfortable to explore it as we wrestle with painful memories, our shortcomings, and the fear of loneliness. But even Jesus's journey included time in a dark cave, and on the other side of that journey was redemption. The good news—in fact, the best news—is that I'm not your ultimate guide. Jesus is. As we journey together, I will help you draw close to him and learn from his example how to live an abundant life.

Now, in case any of this sounds a little dramatic, I assure you that establishing authentic connection is not complicated. I have worked with hundreds of people— married couples, children, teenagers, young adults, and older adults—and have seen all of them improve their relationships and rediscover the joy of being close to those they love. This is what I want for you, and this is what God wants for you.

Thank you for joining me on this journey. I want to help you slam the door on loneliness and build a life full of rich, meaningful relationships that provide a sense of warmth and security for years to come. After finishing this book and the accompanying workbook, I'm confident that you will have the skills you need to make that happen.

This book is meant to be both reflective and interactive. As we consider the five major components of emotional intimacy through the lens of a Catholic therapist, there will be opportunities to reflect and explore your relationships. Each chapter provides ways to help you facilitate and strengthen your relationships through authentic connection. I will include examples from my work in the counseling room along with the practical actions to help you grow in these five areas. It is important to note that the details from these clinical examples have been altered to preserve and protect confidentiality. We will also turn to scripture along the way, for it is surely a light in the darkness! To maximize your experience, I invite you to engage in the exercises within the accompanying workbook and video series. These exercises will deepen and enhance your experience of the five components and help you see measurable results as you seek to reinforce these qualities within your relationships.

What are you waiting for? Grab that flashlight and let's journey into the depths together. I'll be with you every step of the way, and so will Jesus.

The Antidote to Loneliness

Authentic Connection

It is not good for the man to be alone.
—Genesis 2:18

We all know what it's like to feel lonely. Whether you experienced bullying growing up, you have a leadership role, and it's lonely at the top, or you are the last person in your social circle to become married, we've all known the pain of isolation at one point or another.

The worst loneliness I've experienced was during my eight-plus years of infertility. My husband and I yearned to grow our family and despite the countless tests, medications, blood draws, and doctor's appointments, nothing seemed to be working. Watching my close friends, especially ones that were married after us, become pregnant developed into an overwhelming experience. On the one hand, I was happy for my friends. On the other hand, their lives were a reminder of what I'd hoped to experience before time ran out.

Infertility is a traumatic experience. Your body betrays you. Your once-healthy self is now problematic. Baby showers were particularly challenging. I remember one in which I focused all my energy into conveying happiness and collapsed into tears the moment I sat in my car when the celebration was over.

When I felt courageous enough to share my anguish with someone, it was sometimes met with awkward silence or, worse, stories about how they knew someone who got pregnant after the same duration of infertility. I do not fault these people, as I know they were well inten-tioned, they love me, and they were trying to provide a sense of hope. What they did not realize was it felt more isolating as it highlighted my uniqueness. Was there no one who could accompany me in this? A part of me ques-tioned if I belonged in the Catholic world. If I was not growing a large family, was there a place for me and my infertility?

During this time, my husband's graduate studies brought us to the Northeast for a couple of years. Not being physically present with constant reminders of child-bearing among my friends was somewhat of a relief. However, we found ourselves in a new city, searching for community.

This became a time of loneliness in our marriage as well. Daniel, my husband, was focused on the demands of graduate school, and I worked until late in the evenings. There was not much time for us to spend together, and we were already trying to heal our infertility.

As we made connections in our new city and people learned about how long we had been married—you know, long enough when you start to wonder when the kids are coming—we endured questions about having kids. Some were prudent enough not to ask, though you could sense a question in the awkward pause after they asked, "How long have you been married?" and "Any kids?" It may seem benign or trivial, but receiving these questions on a regular basis became vexing. It was as if our openness to life and the teachings of the Church was frequently called into question. None of these people meant any harm by their questions, but it was challenging nonetheless.

Where did we fit in? We were young adults, but we were married. All our married friends were busy with child-rearing. We felt we didn't belong in groups for singles our age and we didn't belong in places where married couples were because we had no story to contribute about children. We didn't belong in most young adult groups because we had found our vocations and were pursuing career goals and were not in any particular phase of significant discernment. Something seemed off in these settings, and it was challenging to connect. In those earlier years, I knew less than a handful of people who disclosed struggles with infertility or miscarriage. Most of them eventually carried their pregnancies to term and grew large families. Where did we belong? Who could we connect with during this time?

I eventually decided to have surgery to help us conceive. The conception window after surgery was nine to twelve months. When that window closed, it was crushing. My mental and emotional stability could not sustain being a failed medical experiment. After a period of grieving and healing, we were able to accept God's plan and direction in our life, but I still felt lonely and disconnected.

What provided me relief during those tough years were a few close friends. One is a childhood friend who is now a religious sister. I poured my heart into letter after letter, and she responded with affirming and supportive messages. She cried with me and wrote about how she admired my faith. I did not feel my faith was strong at that time, so her words stuck with me. One of my other close childhood friends, who is married, also provided a kind, listening ear. She did not offer advice or speak to me in platitudes. She sat with me on the phone and in person, and her silent presence made all the difference. It provided space and told me that she accepted me as I was. The third person is someone who I consider a spiritual mother. She played a large role in my reversion to the faith and loved me as her own. We developed a deep friendship as she journeyed with me from high school into my adult years, and she has been a mentor and mother to me in so many ways. She shared spiritual advice and pointed me toward Our Lady as someone who understood my plight. She also has personally experienced infertility and was someone who could speak with real authority into my life about the pain of not having children here on earth. With great reverence for my suffering, she also invited me into deeper levels of intimacy with Jesus.

The friends and community that the Lord placed in my path gave me a sense of belonging. The letters, the listening ears, the tenderness and attunement to my pain, and the spiritual guidance are what kept me connected. Through these people I stayed grafted to the vine of life and love. Those relationships are what helped me move forward in faith and persevere. They helped those pangs of loneliness feel a little less lonely. Even though our experiences were different, they made me feel as if I still had a place. Their actions and tenderness were affirmations sprinkled throughout the years, reminding me that I did belong and that I did still have a place.

Authentic connection is not just a whimsical idea or an ideal notion. It is vital to our existence. Julianne Holt-Lunstad and Timothy Smith in their research at Brigham Young University have identified a strong relationship between physical health and social health. It is easy to focus on physical health because we can often see tangible symptoms. If someone has a broken leg, we are sympathetic to their difficulty walking and may even feel inclined to help. Social isolation, however, is far more elusive and therefore more challenging to offer support when someone is in need.

Holt-Lunstad and Smith's research affirmed the value of human relationships and found that strong, emotional connections are good for us not only emotionally or spiritually but also physically. They discovered that individuals without strong social support more frequently experienced increased inflammation, cognitive decline, obesity, alcoholism, depression, poorer immune health, and even earlier death. To help give perspective, Holt-Lunstad and Smith say that prolonged periods of loneliness can be as dangerous as smoking a pack of cigarettes a day.

Their research underscores something we all know from experience: friendship and a sense of belonging are essential to our happiness. Through my painful experience of infertility, the Lord shined a light on the need to strengthen my relationships. Then he provided a soft landing place in my family and friends that gave me a sense of belonging and acceptance. This protected against the negative impact of trauma, insecurity, self-doubt, and low self-esteem.

These two things, closeness and belonging, are the major components of connection. When they are present, they make everything better. This is what keeps you coming back to your favorite bar, your CrossFit gym, your church, and your friends. It means you have a place, you belong, and that people notice when you're there or not. You share a closeness with the other people that is made possible by a mutual and intimate knowledge of one another.

If you think back to middle school or high school, you probably experienced something similar to my experience when you tried to find a group. You wanted to belong and to know that there was a sense of closeness with the others there—that they cared about you. You didn't want to be lonely. This basic desire doesn't change as we grow older, but we either find emotional intimacy through real connection or we go on looking for it, whether we realize it or not. This explains why adults can tolerate abusive friendships and romantic relationships when everyone else can see the writing on the wall.

Connection is foundational to emotional intimacy and overcoming loneliness because human beings simply need connection. We thrive when we feel connected with others, and we languish without it. Connection is so important that infants can die from a lack of it. This was discovered in twentieth-century orphanages in places such as China and Romania, when extreme poverty drove many parents to place their children in the care of these institutions. Faced with more children than they could compassionately care for, the nurses were barely able to feed, change, and clothe the children, much less hold, cuddle, and soothe them. As a result, many children died from a lack of human connection. Those who survived often demonstrated severe cognitive or emotional impairments. Human beings need connection.

Increasingly, the world is a lonely place devoid of real connection. Historically it was the elderly who reported feeling the loneliest, and this had something to do, no doubt, with the loss of friends and loved ones, children and grandchildren moving away or being distant, and the type of relational isolation that comes with growing old. However, survey data collected during the COVID-19 pandemic show that young people (middle school into college) have surprisingly replaced older people as the loneliest generation. As we see the loneliness statistics increase, we see corresponding increases in suicide, anxiety, depression, and mental health diagnoses. Even in a digitally connected world, authentic connection is sorely needed.

You read in the introduction that we are made for relationships and self-gift. When we live in accord with the divine plan, we fulfill our destiny of being an icon of God. No wonder connection is so essential. When you consider the Church, the community of people who profess belief in Jesus Christ, you can see how much God desires us to enjoy authentic connection with others. Jesus was insistent that his message was meant for everyone, even the outcasts of society (Lk 5:32, "I have not come to call the righteous to repentance but sinners") and those deemed of little value (Mt 19:14, "Let the children come to me"). Though it took some time, the first Christians, whose growth and growing pains are documented in the Acts of the Apostles, recognized that the Church must be a place of connection, a place of belonging and closeness among her members.

The Eucharist, the source and summit of our faith, could almost be called the sacrament of connection. As a sacrament, it is a source of closeness and belonging. When we receive Jesus in the Eucharist, we are as close to him as it gets. By receiving him, we renew our covenant with the Father and his Church, thereby reaffirming our belonging in his family. The Eucharist is also the ordinary means of forgiveness of venial sins, so when we receive Jesus, we strengthen and renew our connection to him and the other members of the Body.

Human beings need and deserve connection. God wants all of us to be connected, feel close to one another, and have a place to belong. He also emphatically does not want us to feel lonely, and connection with others is part of the antidote. So, let's talk about how to build stronger, healthier connections with the people in your life.

Establishing Connection

"I don't know my kids, and I don't have a lot of time left."

Louis sat across from me for our first session with a serene face. He was retired from the military and came to me because he wanted more out of his relationships, especially with his children. Twenty years, multiple deployments, and a career of demanding assignments meant that he had missed a lot. While no one would fault him for this, the reality was that he simply had not invested time in establishing connections with his children. In many ways, he even felt like he didn't belong in his family.

His three children—two daughters and a son—were seventeen, fifteen, and ten. When he said he didn't have a lot of time, he really meant time with his two older girls, with one leaving for college in less than a year and the other soon to follow.

I looked at him and saw a man who was both serious and desperate—not in the sense of someone who was out of options but in the sense that I knew he would pour himself into whatever I suggested. Smiling, I began to explain the idea of a relationship road map.

Relationship Road Maps

My favorite way to help people understand emotional intimacy is through the concept of relationship road maps.

I've adapted this idea from the concept of "love maps," a term coined by leading relationship researcher Dr. John Gottman. Here is how they work: If you take out a paper map or pull up one on your phone, you will see that those maps are full of detailed information. The details tell you a lot about the terrain, help you identify key landmarks, and allow you to orient yourself. There is seemingly way more than anyone would need to know until that one moment when you realize you need to take a detour to avoid a closed mountain road or sudden traffic jam. That's when you are grateful for the detailed map!

Similarly, a relationship road map is a detailed mental representation of everything you know about someone, especially their inner world. What are their likes and dislikes? What are their favorite restaurants? Who do they have conflict with at their place of work? What hobbies are they currently interested in? Who are their best friends? Do you share secrets and inside jokes? Knowledge of these personal details is one of the things that allows people to feel close. The more detailed your map, the more solid a friendship you are likely to have.

If you aren't sure if you have strong road maps, try this activity. Imagine you had to draw and illustrate a map that represented your relationship with your friend or loved one. How detailed would it be? Could you use it to navigate your interactions with them? Would it be rich with information? Is it up to date? I mean really up to date, like Google-driving-around-with-cameras-on-their-cars up to date? Could you use it well or would you struggle with it? If you answered yes to all but the last question, it sounds like you have a good road map. If not, it might be time to update it.

As I explained all of this to Louis, his expressions softened and he relaxed. Hope appeared on his face for the first time. I could see that he was following me, so I started to ask him about his children. What were their hobbies, passions, and interests? Who were their friends at school? Who were their favorite teachers? What music did they love? How did they view their relationship with God? As you might have guessed, he couldn't answer these questions to his satisfaction.

I soon learned that his oldest, Corinne, was the most like him—or at least she used to be. They used to both be really into classic soul, the music Louis had grown up listening to, but he admitted he didn't know what kind of music she liked these days. They also both used to enjoy trying the many barbecued meats in the open-air markets near a former base, but soon after starting high school she had decided to eat a plant-based diet. Having lost two of his strongest commonalities with her, he didn't know where to begin.

His next daughter, Rebecca, was different. While Louis had never had a hard time staying in shape, he wasn't really into sports. Rebecca lived for lacrosse and was hoping to play in college. Her mom had been the primary driver behind this passion, as Louis was always too busy or not around to take her to practice. Mother and daughter had bonded over sports. More importantly, Rebecca was the empathetic and supportive one in the family. Mature beyond her years, she had stepped up big time and helped out the family when Louis was deployed. Louis felt like he had almost no common ground to start with and was a little afraid that Rebecca resented him for missing so much of her life while also causing her to take on too much responsibility.

Devon, his youngest child and only son, was easier. He still idolized his dad and wanted to be around him, but Louis found it hard at times to deal with his son's nonstop questions. Accustomed to giving orders and receiving a "Yessir" response, he wasn't prepared for his son to respond to everything Louis said with "Why?" If he was honest, he found his son annoying, and he didn't always enjoy being around him. I could tell that it pained him to admit this to me, but I assured him that he didn't need to be ashamed of his feelings, and that we would work on all these things.

"So, how do I get started?" he asked.

Updating Road Maps

Updating and elaborating relationship road maps is one of the easiest ways to build a stronger connection and increase emotional intimacy. If you have ever seen those books of conversation starters or question banks online, they are usually designed to help you develop a more intimate knowledge of the other. If you look in the appendix to this book, you will find a list of questions that you could start with. These are the same sort of questions you probably stayed up late discussing with your siblings or best friends, either on the phone or at a sleepover, and what allowed you to establish such meaningful relationships. The best questions are open-ended, and the topics can range from serious to simple, from shallow to deep. Don't underestimate the importance of knowing someone's favorite fast-food restaurant or rom-com; and don't be afraid to ask about their favorite philosopher, most difficult moment, or what makes them cry. It is just as important to know the good and the bad, the mundane and the mosaic.

For Louis, we created a plan to address the weakest points in each relationship. For his oldest daughter, we decided to develop his relationship road map through rediscovery. One idea Louis decided to try was going on a vegan "restaurant crawl" with Corinne. During that time, he planned to ask her about why eating a plant-based diet was important to her. Just like they used to sample barbecue, they could sample various vegan items, then rank and score them to decide on their favorite. This would eventually become an opportunity to create new memories and new inside jokes. He later shared with me that his daughter liked to bring up how funny his face looked the first time he tried tofu; he couldn't get it down without grimacing. As they continued trying new foods, Louis and Corinne found it easier to be vulnerable and share. Their relationship road maps gradually expanded and became richer, more detailed.

Building a Culture of Warmth and Gratitude

When two people in a relationship lose their sense of warmth and admiration for each other, criticism can creep in. This was the sense Louis had regarding his middle child, Rebecca. He was concerned her maturity was masking resentment, so we decided a transparent approach would help. Research on relationship dynamics has revealed that people in healthy relationships express a minimum of five positive interactions to every one negative interaction. Too many negative comments and you come across like you can't stand the person. Too few and they start to wonder if you can help them grow. We knew that Louis was in a deep hole of negative interactions with Rebecca, so we created a plan to balance that out.

Gratitude is the antidote to resentment and is also a great way to foster warmth and admiration. Try this quick test: How quickly can you come up with five things someone has done for you or about that person for which you are grateful? How about ten? When is the last time you expressed gratitude for one of those things—or for anything? If it's been more than a day, that's too long!

I recommend that people make a daily habit of expressing gratitude to their friends and loved ones. If I can co-opt the phrase frequently seen in airports and subways about suspicious behavior: "If you see something, say something!" It is so helpful to catch people doing good rather than bad! Nothing says "You matter to me" better than specifically and directly acknowledging that you are grateful for something another person did. I say "specifically" because there is something magical about telling people exactly what you appreciate. In educational settings, if you give general, nonspecific praise, people don't know what they are doing that elicited the praise and often don't learn as well. If they don't know what they did, maybe they think you don't really know either! If you've ever had a teacher give you generic and bland yet positive comments on a writing assignment, you know what I am talking about! You know that they didn't read it and that their words of praise are hollow.

Louis realized he no longer took the time to express things like "I'm proud of the young woman you are" or "I like how you always laugh when you feel nervous," so he resolved to fix that. Rebecca turned out to be a tough nut to crack. She would either ignore Louis's comments or roll her eyes. She laughed once and said, "Dad! Why are you being so weird?! *Stop!*" But Louis persisted in catching her doing good, acknowledging her gifts, publicly thanking and praising her, and telling her how much he loved her even when she hadn't done anything remarkable. Eventually she began to open up and reciprocate the affirmations. He told me at one session that she had recently expressed how much she admired his fidelity, loyalty, and courage, and that she tried to emulate those same qualities at home.

Though they had more to do to deepen their connection, Louis's commitment to rebuilding their relationship had already started to strengthen the father-daughter bond.

A 2018 study from The Ohio State University tracked seven hundred families as their daughters grew from first through fifth grade. They asked the parents and daughters to rate their levels of loneliness at various points throughout the years. The study found that, overall, girls' sense of loneliness decreases as they become more confident socially and develop friendships. However, for girls who had fathers who were close and paid attention to their feelings, their rates of loneliness declined much quicker than those who did not have close relationships with their fathers. Louis reestablishing his connection with Rebecca helped to reduce the conflict and loneliness between them.

Remembering the Good Times

You have likely had more good times with your loved ones and friends than you realize. As life gets busy, it is often too easy to forget about the good times. I find this is especially true in people who have known each other for ten years or more and who have not diligently maintained their road maps. I also frequently see it in parents who are exhausted and burned out. Luckily the antidote to this one is simple. When we take time to recall our favorite memories of time spent with others, we see again the near-infinite reasons for loving these people. When it came to Louis working with his ten-year-old son, I invited him to find time with Devon to reflect on their favorite memories together. Louis admitted that this would be a little awkward, so I suggested that he start by having conversations with the whole family to get comfortable. The holidays were approaching, which provided an opportunity while the family was eating dinner together for Louis to ask, "What's one of your favorite Christmas memories? What would you say was the best Christmas we've had together?" This turned into a conversation full of laughter as meaningful moments were recalled.

This worked, and Louis soon found ways to have these types of conversations with his son as they did projects around the house.

There are many ways you can remember the good times together. For friends, this may mean thinking back to when you were in school (or earlier in school) or when you first met. For parents and children, this could mean discussing your favorite family trips or holiday celebrations. For couples, the opportunities include all the above and more—children being born, first dates, proposals, silly stories, burnt meals, and so forth. A story my husband and I like to laugh about is from the first couple months of our marriage. I didn't grow up eating a lot of red meat, so I didn't know the difference between a T-bone steak and a pot roast. One day I spotted a deal on what I thought was a beautiful piece of steak. I bought it and proudly served it up for my husband. He ate it gratefully and probably even had seconds, but he later confided in me that he didn't enjoy pot roast and hoped that I would never make it again. It's silly, but it makes us laugh, and that is why it is a cherished memory.

As you practice recalling the good times, you will realize how natural it is, especially for friends. One of the fruits of any relationship is not just the good times you have in the present but the warmth and joy that you can find in reminiscing about the moments you have shared. You also don't have to engage in this activity too often to reap its benefits. I find that creating a weekly habit out of it helps, especially for those who are busy and struggle to find time for deep conversation. Remembering the good times helped Louis to be more receptive to Devon's natural curiosity and mollified Louis's feelings of frustration when they interacted with each other. The overall effect was that they learned to enjoy spending time together, creating more memories and good times and fortifying their relationship for the future.

The Beginning

Trust and Vulnerability

> The springs of divine power gush forth precisely in the midst of human weakness. Those who share in the sufferings of Christ preserve in their own sufferings a very special particle of the infinite treasure of the world's Redemption, and can share this treasure with others.
> — Pope St. John Paul II
> *On the Christian Meaning of Human Suffering*

On your journey toward authentic connection, you will face dragons. One of the most feared among them is vulnerability. Rightfully so. Vulnerability exposes you to real harm. When you are vulnerable, people can and will hurt you. While our own experience confirms this, here is a story that will help you understand the real risk that vulnerability incurs.

I once met a young man named Mason who had been through a lot. In high school, Mason had been a hardworking kid, hard enough that he had secured some scholarships and, with his parents' help, would be able to afford college without taking on debt. As graduation approached, he was excited to move on to the next stage, make his family proud, and pursue his dream of becoming an engineer.

Mason was not a stranger to tragedy. While in high school, he had already been through the loss of his father due to cancer. Though still grieving, he and his family pushed through the sadness and difficulty of surviving financially as a single-parent household. Mason and his brother, who was one year older, had even taken on part-time jobs to help his mother cover the bills. Naturally his prospects to become an engineer were a source of great hope for everyone.

Shortly after graduating from high school, he lost his mother in a tragic car accident. What should have been a time of celebration and transitioning into an exciting new chapter became a period of even deeper grieving and sadness. Despite this, Mason managed to keep it together as he and his brother prepared to depart for the same college in the fall. They had received enough inheritance money to cover whatever costs they would need, and while this was certainly not the way Mason had hoped to pay for college, he was grateful that his parents had planned for such a scenario.

The first semester went by well enough. Mason and his brother made new friends, excelled academically, and tried to live a typical college life. Mason had always been an easygoing and likable guy, and the loss of his parents hadn't changed that. After completing the fall semester, Mason and his brother returned home to rest and visit with their extended family. Their first Christmas without their parents was emotional, but their close-knit extended family members—cousins, grandparents, aunts, and uncles—were

there for them as they had always been. They were especially excited to hear about the brothers' first semester in
college.

As the start of the spring semester approached, Mason
saw less and less of his older brother. The day before
their planned return to campus, Mason couldn't reach
his brother at all. Eventually his brother texted to say he
was going to stay home for a few extra days and would
catch a ride with someone, telling Mason to go ahead on
his own. "This was odd," Mason admitted to himself, but
he knew that he needed to get back to school and decided
to go ahead anyway.

His brother didn't show up during the first week of
class, and then Mason started to get suspicious. One day
when checking his bank accounts, he was struck with
panic. He had nothing left. Thinking there must be some
mistake, he called his brother to find out what was wrong.
Then he noticed a withdrawal. His brother had taken
everything, leaving nothing of their parents' inheritance
for Mason. He had already paid his tuition for the semester, but now he didn't even have money to buy dinner, let
alone pay rent.

Dumbstruck, Mason couldn't explain what had just
happened to him. He was completely blindsided by this
betrayal. How could his family member do this to him?
Didn't his brother know that he needed that money and
that without it he had nothing? In just a few months
Mason had lost everything. No family, no money, and in
his mind, no future. It was the ultimate betrayal.

For the rest of the semester Mason did whatever he
could to make do. His friends rallied together to support
him, letting him couch surf, do laundry, and study. He ate
lots of ramen noodles and leftover pizza and somehow
found a way to make it through his semester, still with

decent grades. But as the end of the semester approached, Mason knew that he couldn't sustain this for another three years.

He decided to take the summer off, living with a relative and working so that he could save money for the fall semester. But despite his ability to manage the external problems, Mason was not okay on the inside. After the betrayal and without the emotional support of his immediate family, a part of Mason's heart shut down. How could he trust anyone after his brother had stolen from him? Someone who should have been there to help him along had taken everything from him, even his last remaining family tie. "Maybe blood isn't thicker than water after all," Mason thought to himself one day.

After a summer of hard work and more student loans, Mason was able to return to college in the fall. He never let himself become bitter or resentful, but his social life stalled. The friendships he had established during his freshman year were still there, but they never grew stronger. Even if he had wanted to, he didn't think he could ever feel comfortable opening up about what had happened. His friendships provided little joy in his life, as he never felt comfortable being vulnerable with those he was close to.

In his dating life, it was much the same. He went out with several young women that fall, but whenever things started to require more emotional commitment, he withdrew. For their part, the women just thought he was a shallow guy who couldn't commit. This couldn't have been further from the truth, but Mason wouldn't have been able to articulate the problem even if he had wanted to. He had learned a terrible and false truth—that he could never be vulnerable with someone. If he did, they would hurt him.

Afraid to open up, lonely, and grieving, Mason had nothing but the memories of a once-happy family.

Vulnerability and Emotional Intimacy

Without vulnerability, relationships stay in the shallows. Vulnerability is what makes all types of love, friendship, and romance possible. So, what is vulnerability? It means to expose the truth of who you really are to someone else, risking laughter, rejection, judgment, and ridicule while hoping for love, acceptance, and affirmation. To be vulnerable is to be exposed, but to be vulnerable is also to be fully alive. The fullness and richness of relationships, community, and intimacy are born out of the defenselessness of vulnerability.

So, if the reward is so great, why are we so afraid to risk vulnerability? Because we have been hurt in the past! As good as authentic relationships sound, we have built a protective habit that keeps us from being wide open with others. Whenever we have an opportunity to be vulnerable, a voice in our head screams, "Red alert!" Rather than proceed, we shut down and the intimacy that we hoped for is squashed before it has a chance to grow.

Whether this describes you or someone you know, in this chapter I want to help you understand how to be vulnerable. Why? Because vulnerability is necessary to experience connection as God intended. Every relationship can be an experience of the Trinity, but only if we have the courage to be accessible. Of course, courage is easy to come by when the dragons are out of sight. In all honesty, it would be very convenient if vulnerability were not required for authentic connection. So why is it necessary and is there any way other than vulnerability to have a meaningful relationship?

Why It's Necessary

Experiencing emotional intimacy as God intended isn't possible without vulnerability. Why? Emotional intimacy is that relationship quality that lets you feel comfortable allowing another to peer into the depths of your heart and soul. It's what allows you to share profoundly in a sometimes nerve-racking exchange of trust. It is an invitation for someone to journey alongside you in the beautiful complexity of life, sharing in both the joys and pains while you grow in mutual affection.

There is a reason people don't grow close when they just talk about the weather, although when you have great emotional intimacy, you can *just* talk about the weather sometimes. Unless you are willing to risk revealing the truth of who you are to someone, even in moderation, your connection will rarely progress and grow deeper. This isn't good or bad; it's just how things are. The *stuff* that relationships are built on comes from inside, and you must be vulnerable to share that type of stuff. Just as it's futile to try to stay dry if you want to play in the ocean, you can't enjoy emotional intimacy without vulnerability. Vulnerability has additional psychological benefits. Being courageous in a sensitive moment creates space for you to recognize and relish different aspects of yourself.

This doesn't mean that you must share recklessly. Not everyone deserves to know everything—the good and the bad—that has happened in your life, and most people won't need to know much at all. But the closer people are, and the closer you want them to be, the more you need to be willing to share yourself with them.

When I met Mason, he was starving for emotional intimacy, especially since he had lost both parents and a close sibling relationship. His lack of emotional intimacy was because he was simply unwilling to be vulnerable. Mason found time and time again that his dating relationships would come to an end because there was a threshold of vulnerability he could not cross. To do so would have put him in a position to be hurt, rejected, and abandoned all over again. To these women, it was as if Mason was saying that he wasn't ready to take their relationship to the next level. They saw no future with him, and they questioned how much he actually cared about them. His friendships and romantic attachments could only go so far without Mason exposing himself as he truly was, and this meant that he could never experience the emotional intimacy he was craving.

Without vulnerability, loneliness prevails and creates more separation and disconnect in our relationships. I may even go so far as to say that vulnerability is the ultimate difference between feeling lonely and feeling connected. It is quintessential, the lynchpin, the single thread that ties and holds relationships together. It permeates every strong bond and connection.

Is There Another Way?

There's no way around this one: we desire connection. While this might seem like a problem, it's actually good news. We believe in a triune God who is connection. God reveals himself as Father, Son, and Spirit; and we are made in his image and likeness, so we too are meant to exist in connection. We often speak of the Church as being the family of God, the *Body* of Christ, and the *Communion* of Saints. We were designed to love and be loved because we are a living image of a God who is love, communion, and connection. We become more of who we were meant to be when we develop rich, meaningful, deep, and vulnerable relationships that are ripe with emotional intimacy. We are more fully alive when we experience authentic connection. As tough as it may be, vulnerability is the path to experiencing relationships and connection as God intended.

So how do we know we should be vulnerable? Examples of vulnerability abound in our faith, and the greatest proof of all is the life of Jesus. God himself became vulnerable to love us in the person of Christ. He was vulnerable as a child raised in a human family. He was vulnerable with his friends and enemies, opening himself up to rejection and betrayal. He was vulnerable still more when he gave his life for us on the Cross, and he continues to be vulnerable daily in the Eucharist, just so that he can be close to us.

So, yes, God invites us to be vulnerable so that we can connect with others and be who we are created to be. The problem is that when we do this, we expose ourselves to be hurt. Families and friends do not always love us perfectly, and we rescind our vulnerability to prevent further hurt. In the extreme, this can lead to emotional isolation. For all of us, our fear of vulnerability can hold us back from living according to God's plan for us. What are we to do? The very thing we have learned to do to protect ourselves from pain is the thing that keeps us from experiencing togetherness.

Learning, Then Unlearning Your Defense Mechanisms

Imagine yourself as a child who was verbally and emotionally manipulated by your parents growing up. Imagine being held responsible for the emotional state of one or both parents. Your mom might have blamed you for her feeling sad or unhappy. Maybe your father gave you the silent treatment when he was angry. Perhaps one or both of your parents were passive-aggressive and you didn't know what to expect; you just knew you had to find a way to soothe and calm them until they were in a good mood again.

Children who live this way are forced to learn the necessary skills to survive in an unhealthy family culture. They learn to adapt and adjust in ways no child should have to. They master the art of keeping the peace in the home and avoiding blame or punishment. This takes a lot of patience and foresight, especially for a child. As you might guess, these children also learn to hide anything that can make them vulnerable, safeguarding themselves from additional pain.

When children from such an environment become adults, their survival skills don't always help them to adapt successfully. In friendship, you might question if someone genuinely cares about you or if they are just tolerating you out of pity. You might think that another person doesn't value your friendship when you see them investing time in other relationships. You wonder, "Didn't I do enough to make this friendship a priority?" If too much time goes by between phone calls or texts, you might start asking yourself if you have done something wrong. Even in situations where a friend does something hurtful, the fear of being vulnerable usually stops any attempts at reconciliation before they begin.

Before trigger warnings became commonplace, the term *trigger* had a technical meaning in the world of therapy to describe thoughts, emotions, memories, and sensations from the past that cause involuntary responses, reactivating past hurts, wounds, and trauma. Even in a different context than the initial trauma, triggered emotions can wash over you in a moment, leaving panic and fear in their wake. When this happens, the last thing you are likely to do is show vulnerability. The coping strategies that you learned at an early age, brought on by such things as a caregiver's betrayal, take over and guide the internal monologue and behavior of the individual in the present moment.

In and of themselves, these coping strategies aren't a bad thing. They are our emotional system's approach to creating a map of the world that has two sections: safe and unsafe. Anything that registers a terrible emotional response gets labeled as unsafe. Whenever we encounter anything that closely resembles that unsafe section of the map, a trigger, our emergency protection system kicks in to keep us safe. But while the mapping system is good, sometimes it isn't always accurate. Things that should be safe, like close relationships, can be labeled as unsafe when people hurt us.

The key to overcoming our fear of vulnerability is to learn our triggers—those things that cause fear and anxiety to overwhelm us—and gradually relearn how to interpret those triggers. While this might sound intimidating, I have helped many people—single adults, married folks, and senior citizens—develop the ability to show more vulnerability. As a result, they enjoy better relationships with richer, more meaningful connections.

Identify Your Triggers

First of all, you must be able to recognize the moments that create that sense of discomfort. This discomfort can show up in the form of strong emotions such as anger, rage, sadness, or withdrawal. It can manifest as a surge of adrenaline, muscle tension, or rapid shallow breathing. Sometimes it presents as worrisome, intrusive, or cyclical thoughts.

If you are unsure about what your triggers are, it can be helpful to journal or log times when you notice things like strong emotions, muscle tension, or irritability. Pay attention to details, such as time of day or activities you engaged in when these signs occurred. After logging this information for one to two weeks, you may begin to notice a pattern. For example, if you experience irritability on staff-meeting days or anxiety every evening just before bed, that's a good indication something is triggering you.

You can keep your own log in the accompanying workbook. I've created a template there to help get you started that makes it easy to select what signs you can track for yourself.

One thing that may surprise you is just how many things can be considered a trigger. If you were hoping for a list, it would be endless! Triggers are any experience, whether sensory, chronological, emotional, and beyond, that we associate with a painful memory. For some of my clients, they have discovered that their triggers were something as simple as the smell of hand sanitizer in a hospital, the taste of a food that reminds them of a person or event, or the date of an impactful memory. Why is this important? Because I don't want you to overlook or dismiss a triggering moment. As you begin to log times of emotional stress or discomfort, you might be tempted to minimize your own triggers because they don't seem big enough. I frequently hear this concern being expressed. Many say that their situation isn't "bad enough" for them to justify being disconcerted. If it's not the sound of a gunshot, an aggressive dog barking, or being in the physical presence of someone who hurt you, you might think that it would not (or should not) be powerful enough to trigger a sense of protectiveness during a vulnerable moment. But all that is happening is your brain is showing its ways to prevent you from being hurt again. We unintentionally and significantly underestimate the power of our brain's ability to protect us.

One reason why the brain so easily associates simple experiences, like scents or calendar dates, with pain is to keep us from exposing ourselves to danger again. The challenge that we have is that sometimes our brain is overprotective. Things that are not actually dangerous are perceived incorrectly as threats. One of my close friends once shared that because he was involved in an accident while driving a popular sport-utility vehicle, he is frequently triggered by other cars made by that manufacturer. Obviously, not every one of those cars is a threat, but his brain still doesn't recognize that. Anytime he sees those cars on the road, he is reminded of his accident and feels a small but very real sense of dread. He even would notice himself driving more carefully from time to time when near those types of cars.

Triggers can also build and compound on one another to culminate in an exaggerated response separate from the time of the triggering event all together. For example, let's look at Iris's experience of discovering her own triggers gradually. Iris had always been a sensitive and introspective person, prone to overthinking and anxiety. She had a keen sense of intuition and often picked up on subtleties that others missed. However, her heightened awareness of the world around her also made her vulnerable to feeling overwhelmed by the slightest triggers.

One day, as Iris was walking to work, the sound of jackhammers from a nearby construction site startled her. She felt her heart rate increase, her palms sweat, and her thoughts spiral out of control. She couldn't understand why the noise affected her so much, but she couldn't shake the feeling of unease. Later that day, Iris was in a meeting with her boss when he made a comment about her work that she perceived as critical. Her anxiety spiked again, and she struggled to focus on the rest of the meeting. She replayed the comment in her mind over and over, obsessing over every detail and second-guessing her abilities. As the days went on, Iris began to notice other triggers that affected her mood and behavior. The smell of certain foods, the sight of certain colors, and even the tone of someone's voice could all have an impact on her emotional state.

Through therapy and self-reflection, Iris came to understand that her heightened sensitivity and introspection were both a blessing and a curse. While she had a unique ability to empathize with others and pick up on subtle cues, she was also more susceptible to feeling overwhelmed by the world around her. By acknowledging and embracing her experiences, Iris was able to manage her anxiety more effectively and lead a more fulfilling life.

The same could be true for you.

Identifying your triggers is an essential step because unless you understand what is causing the negative emotional or physical response, you won't be able to retrain your body's response to that stimulus. I often see people in therapy who thought that they could broadly apply relaxation or stress-reduction techniques. But these only work when they are done as a response to the trigger. Without a target to aim at, they never understand when to take a shot!

Develop a Strategy for Your Triggers

Once you identify your triggers, develop a planned response. Mason and I created such a strategy. After spending a few weeks journaling about his emotional responses, Mason noticed that his jaw became clenched when he was triggered. This also helped clear up why he had been experiencing jaw pain and toothaches off and on for several months. Anytime he noticed his jaw tightening, he knew that he was in a triggering situation.

Per our plan, anytime Mason noticed his jaw clenching, he would pause and intentionally relax his jaw. If this step was too difficult, Mason would take slow, deep breaths, tensing his jaw during the inhale and relaxing it during the exhale.

We also discovered from his log that making decisions was a big trigger for Mason. To help prevent a swell of negative emotions when he needed to make a serious decision about dating or relationships, we developed a calming routine using guided reflections. The result was that he approached such decisions from a place of peace rather than with a strained physiological response.

You can create a plan for yourself just like Mason's. If you don't experience muscle tension, there are other ways you can notice a triggered response. For example, your mind starts racing or you become tired or irritable at a particular moment. Keeping a log of your symptoms is crucial toward identifying what occurs for you specifically. Write everything down, even if it seems irrelevant or minimally important. Sometimes it's helpful to begin with any strong or negative emotion and see what patterns develop over a few weeks.

Self-soothing techniques like the ones Mason used help dampen the fight-flight-or-freeze response that can happen when you are triggered. Calming down is essential because there are often lies hidden in the unwelcome, racing, or anxious thoughts that accompany negative emotions. By self-soothing, you will have the mental clarity to scrutinize your thoughts, identify any falsehoods within, and then rewrite your internal monologue so that it reflects the truth.

What do these lies sound like? Let's say you had a falling out with your best friend in college and haven't spoken in several years. One day when you go to your boyfriend's house (or girlfriend's house, if you are male), you see that former best friend getting out of a moving truck, only to find out that she is moving in across the street from your boyfriend. This triggers you; you start to feel very anxious and uncomfortable. But you have been studying your triggers, so you start to do box breathing, a breathing exercise you learned recently. As you do this and your heart rate lowers, you may recognize your inner narrative. "She moved here just to spite me. Now she is going to make my life miserable every time I come over. This will ruin things with my boyfriend and I'll have to break up with him!" you hear yourself saying. But since you are calm, you can recognize that those thoughts aren't true. Did she really move here just to spite you? "Probably not," you tell yourself. "How could she have known my boyfriend lives here?" Do you have to leave? "No, I don't have to leave. I can be here too." And so you rewrite your inner monologue to be healthier, more representative of reality.

Once you know approaches to calm yourself, create a plan and practice it. First, just practice on your own, in private. Try saying something like, "I notice my jaw is clenched . . ." even if it isn't, and then go into your routine. By practicing in this way, your planned response to stress will come a little more naturally in actual stressful situations.

Practice

The next step is to slowly reintroduce moments of vulnerability in order to build a higher stress tolerance. You will need to start small and rehearse being vulnerable in safe ways before gradually building up to situations that require more and more vulnerability. For example, Mason tried asking an awkward question to a store clerk or stranger, knowing that he was not likely to ever see that person again. That was a comfortable place for him to start; for you it may be different. Perhaps you would be more comfortable talking with your most trusted friend or family member. I often recommend planning for these moments in a therapeutic setting to ensure you are not opening yourself up to further emotional damage while practicing. Working with triggers can be unpredictable, highly emotional, and challenging at times. Sometimes there are Pandora's box moments where everything comes to the surface. A clinical professional is trained to ensure you are mentally, emotionally, and physically safe while navigating your triggers.

Ask Yourself, "What Would I Do in This Situation If I Had Not Been Hurt in the Past?"

Ask yourself, "What would I do in this situation if I had not been hurt in the past?" The answer to that question is not how you should act every time you are in that situation but rather a helpful guide for what you want to work up to. Questions like this also help you decide if this is an appropriate time to practice vulnerability. If the answer to the question doesn't trigger you, you might be ready to take the next step forward.

After practicing for several weeks, Mason felt comfortable trying this in his dating life. When a woman asked him a personal question that made him uncomfortable, he noticed his jaw clenching shut. This was an indicator for Mason to ask himself, "How would I answer this question if I had not been hurt by my brother in the past?" That gave Mason the courage to risk answering that and other questions he might otherwise have avoided and allowed him to share more than he ever had. His dating life became much more stable and intentional after this one exchange.

In other situations, you could ask yourself, "How would I respond to a friend ignoring my texts if I had not been hurt in the past?" Or "If I risk and share how I'm feeling in this moment, what do I stand to gain? How would this relationship grow?" These are questions you can ask to move yourself toward deepening your emotional connection and ability to be vulnerable with others.

Jesus, Emotional Intimacy, and the Fulfillment of Our Desire

As disciples of Jesus, we look to him as the model for our own life. His teachings are echoed in the way he lived and loved, and when we follow his words and actions, we find a plan for our life that leads us into the inner life of the Trinity. In Jesus's relationships we can see vulnerable intimacy—the way he shared his life with others, trusted them, expressed vulnerability, and gave to them his whole self. We can pattern our relationships on his example.

Jesus enjoyed profound close relationships with a select few of his disciples. This is surprising given his mission to save the whole world, but in this mystery he reveals how we are supposed to live the Gospel. We are not meant for many superficial relationships but for stable, long-term, profound relationships. Let us not be afraid to go there too!

Among Jesus's closest friends were the siblings Martha, Mary, and Lazarus. Though they are mentioned little in the Gospel, it appears that he shared a special friendship with them. In a famous passage, we see Martha playing host while Mary sits comfortably at the feet of Jesus, soaking up his wisdom. Martha knew Jesus well enough to believe that he would raise her brother, Lazarus, in the age to come and that Jesus could have saved Lazarus from death if he had come earlier (Jn 11:24; 21). Upon finding that Lazarus had died, Jesus was moved to tears (Jn 11:35), and this passage reads like a description of a friend who is weeping over the death of someone dear to him, not just a pious expression of sentiment over a tragedy. What vulnerability for God to cry in front of those whom he was sent to save! What trust! Jesus really made space in his heart to care about people such that he was heartbroken when Lazarus died, and then he let people see it!

Jesus's relationship with the Twelve reveals the emotional intimacy he had with them. He shared secrets with them (Mk 8:27–30), spent more time explaining his teaching (Lk 8:9–15), made himself vulnerable by revealing his inner life (Jn 15:1–17), and trusted them with his safety (Mt 26:36-46). In his relationship with Peter, James, and John, we see that Jesus enjoyed a special intimacy with these three. It was Peter whom he called out of the boat to walk on water (Mt 14:22–33) and to whom he gave the keys of the kingdom (Mt 16:19). It was those three who were with him at the Transfiguration (Mt 17:1–13), and the Gospel even makes it explicit that they were alone (v. 1). Jesus took these three with him into the garden to pray, and again shared his secrets, fears, and inner life with his friends when he said, "My soul is sorrowful even to death. Remain here and keep watch with me" (Mt 26:37–38).

Up to that point, there could have been no more vulnerable moment in Jesus's life than the agony in the garden. I can imagine Jesus grieving, sweating, bleeding, and crying when asking for the cup to pass from him. The only people he asks to join him in that exposed and unguarded moment were Peter, James, and John. He let his friends see all of him. He wished for their support and entrusted them with not only his biggest fears but also with the heights of glory in the Transfiguration. This was not something he showed to everyone, at least not immediately. At this point, it was only shown to those with whom he developed the closest relationship; those with whom he had been vulnerable.

In the greatest example of vulnerability the world has ever known, and one that extends not just to a few friends but to every person who has ever lived, Jesus makes a gift of his entire self in the Eucharist. If intimacy is a sharing of oneself, a closeness with another person, and a revealing of interiority, the Eucharist is intimacy incarnate. In the Eucharist, Jesus offers to make his home in our hearts and invites us to make our home in him so that we could experience the inner life of the Trinity. In this act, he extends to you and me the emotional intimacy that we see manifested in his relationship with his disciples and close friends.

To those for whom vulnerability is a struggle or something you yearn for, the beautiful hope of Christianity is that Jesus is the fulfillment of what we all long for. He offers to share everything with us, making himself vulnerable, drawing near to us, revealing and entrusting himself and his mission to us. In him we find not simply a model for how we should live but the fullness of everything we long for.

In 2 Corinthians, St. Paul writes, "Therefore, I am content with weaknesses, insults, hardships, persecutions, and constraints, for the sake of Christ; for when I am weak, then I am strong" (2 Cor 12: 10). St. Paul is not just saying that our weaknesses allow room for the power of Christ to live and work through us. I believe he is also saying that vulnerability and weakness in and of itself is strength in the same way that Christ's death was power and strength. We

believe in a God who reigns with a glorified and wounded human body. It is through those very wounds that he
heals and saves the whole world. Uniting our wounds to
him, we participate in the ongoing salvation of the world,
even when we put ourselves on the line to establish deeper connection and drive away loneliness. Vulnerability is
the strength and power to connect, love, and unite that no
amount of force, coercion, or cunning can ever approach.

In 2015, another reiteration of *Cinderella* was released. I
was struck by one of the lines included in this version, as
Cinderella is about to reveal her true identity to the prince
and claim the glass slipper. She was nervous about the
prince seeing her in rags and not as the glamorous person
she was on the night they met, and she said to herself,
"Perhaps the greatest risk any of us will ever take is to be
seen as we really are." At that moment, she had a choice
to risk rejection to gain a love like no other.

That is vulnerability. Allowing yourself to be seen as
you truly are, rags and all. To be gazed upon and looked
upon. When we gaze upon the Cross or the Eucharist,
Jesus returns that gaze. He shows us time and time again
throughout his life and relationships what it means to
be exposed and to let someone in. When we do that, the
power of his healing love pours forth, binding people
together in the most unbreakable bond . . . that is ultimately God himself.

3

The Tools

Communicating
during Conflict

The past is never dead. It's not even past.
—William Faulkner
Requiem for a Nun

Past emotional injuries and conflicts that have
not been processed are like a stone in your shoe
. . . we need a way to take the stone out and
process.
—Dr. John Gottman
Level 1 Training, Gottman Method
Couples Therapy

My husband, Daniel, loves to tell the story of the time
he volunteered us for a communication activity. It was
during our marriage preparation retreat, and the presenter, a therapist, had just finished explaining a model of
communication. As soon as she asked for a volunteer,

Daniel's hand shot up into the air. He loves doing things like that and knows that I don't. I tried to become invisible as I saw the grin spread across his face. Of course, the presenter invited us to sit in two chairs in front of about fifty other couples. The last thing I wanted to do was model communication for strangers. But I was studying to be a therapist and had the overconfidence of a graduate student who had it all figured out. How hard could it be?

The rules were simple: Daniel would make a brief statement about something that was frustrating him, but he had to start his sentences with the word *I* and avoid using the word *you*. My job was to repeat back to him what he just said. Then I would ask, "Did I get that?" His job was to confirm that I, the perfect listener, had indeed heard what he said.

He started, "I feel hurt when . . ." I thought I knew what he was talking about, so when he finished, I repeated back what I thought he meant. "Did I get it?" I asked? "No. Let me try again," he said awkwardly. "I feel hurt when . . ." "No way am I going to make a mistake twice," I thought. Again I stated, "What I hear you saying is . . . Did I get it?" "No," he said firmly. The therapist stepped in to give me tips on how to hear what Daniel was sharing and at that moment I could hear some of the couples in the crowd mumbling. Suddenly embarrassed, I couldn't believe that I had failed to understand one simple sentence not once but twice. "Let me try again," he said.

Trying to communicate what we hold true amid conflict is a difficult task. While much of our daily exchanges stay in neutral territories such as weather, sports, and general rhythm-of-life stuff, conflict tends to dive more deeply into meaning, values, dreams, and goals. Conflict can also leave us feeling attacked. We itch to defend ourselves and win the fight. There was certainly a part of me that felt defensive when my soon-to-be-husband expressed a concern about our relationship in a public format. In conflict, we are often so busy trying to refute the other person's idea that we miss the more meaningful subtext: purpose or symbolism.

Let's say a couple is having an argument about money. Perhaps one person is a natural saver and the other is a natural spender. On the surface, this should not be much of an argument. Either you have the money to purchase something or you don't. All it takes is a quick look at the budget and the bank account. However, the reason that conflict about money is so common is because it is an argument about the meaning people attribute to money. Otherwise the conversation would end after some basic math calculations. When a couple is debating about a purchase, the underlying message of that conversation could be about status, financial security, lifestyle, a goal or dream, and so on. When we don't take time to understand the essence of what another person is communicating, we lose an opportunity for connection and often invite more tension into the relationship.

Even when our conversations aren't about finances, sometimes we just don't feel understood, heard, or noticed. Many of my clients share that despite having attentive parents, being in loving relationships, and knowing great friends, they feel as if no one knows the truth of who they really are. They long to convey that truth to someone and for someone to receive and honor the mystery within. Like my clients, many of us don't have the quality relationships that we desire. For one reason or another, we get stuck at a superficial level, discussing the weather and daily happenings but glossing over or forgetting altogether the emotional needs of one another.

Loneliness, in the sense of being in relationship but not feeling seen or heard, is insidious. It creeps in slowly and quietly until finally you realize you're unhappy and emotionally lonely. Even if the picture isn't as grim as the one I just painted, let's ask ourselves a tough question: How satisfied are you with the quality of your most important relationships? Do you enjoy enough emotional intimacy with your spouse, children, parents, siblings, and closest friends? While I enjoy many high-quality relationships, I often find myself wishing I were a little closer to someone, that I had more chances for intimate conversation, and that I could really share who I am. I would be willing to bet you feel the same.

Navigating Conflict

When I first began formulating the ideas for this book, a friend asked me what it would be about. When I mentioned communication as one of the themes, she joked that she and her husband communicated often and easily and teased that there wouldn't be anything worth writing about. "After all, it's just talking, right?" What she was touching on is that on the surface, the act of communication is just an exchange of information. But, for emotional intimacy to flourish and to eradicate loneliness, communication must be an exchange of meaning and values. And when people converse on things they care about, they will inevitably encounter conflict.

It was during that playful conversation with my friend that I realized she had a different interpretation of the term communication than I did. My friend viewed communication as the act of exchanging words. Meaning, if she and her husband had what they considered to be relatively happy and frequent conversation, then that meant there was no issue with their communication. Certainly speaking to one another in and of itself is an important piece to the overall and broader topic of communication. However, as a therapist, when I think about communication, I think about a few different nuances and layers.

Quality vs. Quantity

We can easily see that there's a distinction to be made between *how often* you communicate with someone versus *what* you communicate to someone. While we might experience frequent communication in relationships of all kinds, not all communication is created equal. You might take part in superficial chatter with a friend or hand off marching orders to your spouse. But these moments of "communication" don't usually contribute meaningfully to the growth and depth of the relationship. Couples who only communicate about things like chores, checklists, errands and responsibilities often report lower levels of satisfaction. To grow in emotional intimacy, we need to share our interior lives. This is self-evident for couples, but it is true for all our relationships, at least to the degree that we want to draw closer to others.

Finding opportunities to communicate in a way that is meaningful can be a struggle when life is busy. Maybe you simply can't find the time to ask a friend how their week was or let your spouse know how much you appreciate their sacrifices for the family. But creating these regular touchpoints of quality communication is essential to emotional intimacy. Otherwise, we are running on autopilot and never reflecting on who we are, what our loved ones need from us, and never turning that into meaningful action.

Responsiveness and Receptivity

Once people are sharing in greater depth with one another, two important factors are responsiveness and receptivity.

Think of those times when you were eager to share something with someone close to you but, sadly, they either didn't respond or received your news with tepidity. When we share with someone, we are hoping that they will both respond and receive our news. That is, they give us their attention and welcome our news, showing us that they understand how important it is to us. This can be easily seen in children who share practically everything with their parents, hoping for both response and receptivity. Every new discovery, song, dance move, and artwork is worthy of sharing. As we grow older, it seems we are less and less willing to share in this way. Perhaps this is because we have too frequently been ignored or rebuffed by others when we did try to share.

Each time we make an effort to share with someone, we gamble connection. If we win, we grow closer to the other person. If we lose, we feel more distant. Over the course of months and years, you either build a huge stack of positive experiences, or you hit relationship bankruptcy. While these conversations in themselves might not manifest as a conflict, they often set you up for conflict later down the road. I see this in therapy sessions when people have an emotional outburst towards a friend or family member. This is not usually an isolated incident but rather comes after many desperate attempts to get someone to respond and receive them. In a paradoxical way, conflict can be a solution to these situations. When you recognize that someone else is not responding or receiving, you could engage in a controlled conflict, asking if now is a good time to discuss something or if you should revisit it later. If you are on the other end of this conversation, you might instead say that you recognize someone needs your attention and respond accordingly, or offer to talk another time if you are unable to accommodate them in the moment.

Communicating through Conflict

What kind of therapist would I be if I did not discuss the importance of communication—particularly how communication unfolds in the midst of conflict? When conflict arises in a relationship, which it inevitably does regardless of the type of relationship, the methods of communication used to address the conflict by the parties involved is ultimately what makes the difference between increasing a sense of loneliness or keeping it at bay.

Here's the thing about communicating through conflict: it must be understood that conflict is good! Many people often believe that in order to have healthy relationships, there should never be any conflict, tension, or disagreement. But that is not always the case. It might seem a bit voyeuristic, but as a relationship therapist I look forward to working with people in the midst of their conflict. Not because I get enjoyment out of their temporary misfortune or frustration, but because I know what is possible in the midst of that tension. I know what lies on the other side if they're willing to wade into the discomfort.

Conflict is good for relationships because it provides an opportunity to share hearts, learn more about the other person and grow closer to them. It is a signal that you are *engaging with the other person on a level deep enough to strengthen the relationship.*

We recently decided to watch *Sleeping Beauty* with our four-year-old daughter. It was my first time seeing the film as an adult and it touched me in a new way when reflecting on conflict and relationships. Toward the end of the movie, the prince must overcome many obstacles in order to reach his true love, Princess Aurora. He traverses steep ravines, jumps over collapsing bridges on his horse, and cuts through gnarly, treacherous thorns en route to fighting the evil Maleficent, who has taken the form of a dragon. He braves all these dangers to reach the castle where Aurora is sleeping. He was on a mission and determined to be with the one he loves. No matter how difficult, it was as if nothing could stop him.

That is the attitude we need to bring to our conflicts. Sure, it's safe and comfortable in the cottage in the woods. But life there will be boring and unsatisfying, and we know we are called beyond. This unmet desire for deeper purpose and risk bubbles up whether we like it or not. If you've ever witnessed a friendship fall apart over what seemed like a minor offense, there's a good chance that someone was unwilling to address an insult early on. That insult festered until it was strong enough to break the bonds of friendship, and that doesn't have to happen. What I want is for you to feel comfortable having difficult conversations knowing that if the other person is of good will, you can come out of the conflict stronger, closer, and better off.

In the pages that follow, we are going to learn how to navigate conflict confidently and successfully. If you want to develop emotional intimacy, you will necessarily engage in conflict. I know that sounds strange, but I see this in my office every day because people have persistent personality differences and divergent desires. If you spend more than a trivial amount of time with others, these differences will come up, and you will eventually disagree. That disagreement can lead to greater emotional intimacy but only if you embrace a selfless approach to communication. Why? Because conflict gives the members of a relationship the opportunity to reciprocate selflessness, and that can only strengthen a relationship. The communication and conflict strategies in this chapter work when people are willing to put on Christ in their interactions and look first to the good of the other. So let's talk about how you can handle conflict so that it leads you toward connection and away from loneliness.

Learning to Validate

When someone you care for is suffering, you want to help, right? There are at least two ways I can think of to help. First, you can take away the pain. This works sometimes, but not always. You can remove splinters, bandage cuts, and ice sprained ankles, but it's hard to fix everything. Recently my family was planning to visit an amusement park. We told our young daughter about it and she was so excited to go. Then I tested positive for COVID-19. I had to explain to her why we couldn't go, and naturally she was upset. No amount of explaining, reasoning, or arguing was going to change that. There was nothing to fix.

When you can't fix someone's suffering, you can acknowledge it, empathize, and accompany them. When my husband heard our daughter crying, he came into the room and began to validate her feelings by saying, "You are really upset, aren't you?" "Yes!" she sobbed. He continued with simple questions that let her know he understood how upset she was and within a few moments, she was calm again.

Is it right to cry about not being able to go to a theme park? Yes . . . no . . . maybe? But does it matter? When someone is upset, you don't first ask if it's rational for that person to be upset. You comfort them! That's why the rule of validity is so important, and it applies to adults just as much as it does to children. Even if the people we love are upset for irrational reasons, the important thing is often the fact that they are upset. In many cases, what they need is a hug, not an explanation.

For conflict to become an opportunity for greater intimacy, you first need to be able to see the other person's experience as valid. This is different from being right. It's more about acknowledging reality as it is. In the case of the theme park trip with my daughter, the reality was that she was sad, and I care about that. In conflicts with friends, family, and loved ones, the other person's experience is real and they probably want you to care about it. If they think you care, they no longer must try to convince you of that. This sense of understanding creates a safe environment for real communication.

One essential step is to try to withdraw from your position and look at the big picture. If you've ever had the experience of witnessing an argument and thinking that the people involved were acting immature, you know what it is to look at the big picture. Or consider what it's like to watch replays of live sporting events with multiple camera angles, high-definition cameras, and slow motion. You can be way more objective than the players who had a limited view of the event and who are far more invested than you are. When we learn to step back and see the big picture in our conflicts, we develop a superpower.

Practically, how do we do this? It means taking a minute to walk in someone else's shoes, imagining yourself in the other person's physical, mental, and emotional state of mind. This requires some practice and imagination, but I have seen it work wonders for people engaged in conflict. A spirit of empathy and accompaniment usually provides people with a deeper understanding of the other person's perspective, allowing them to feel a sense of solidarity with the other.

Empathy is the capacity to understand someone else's feelings, thoughts, and experiences from their point of reference. I believe it is an act of charity to show empathy. Your attentiveness honors their dignity because by taking the time to notice them, you are sending a clear message that you value the other person. You are saying they are worthy of your time and attention. If you aren't sure how they feel, you can ask, or you can use a phrase like "It sounds like you are feeling frustrated." If you are right, they will appreciate it. If you are wrong, you have given them space and permission to share more about how they really feel. That allows you to express your empathy, which you can do with statements like "That makes sense," "You're in a tough spot," or "No wonder you're upset."

Here's an important caveat: Saying that another person's point of view is valid does not mean that you agree with them. It does not mean that you admit that they are right and you are wrong. It simply means that you paused to get inside their head and understand why they feel the way they feel.

Seeing someone's viewpoint as valid is part of seeing the bigger picture. If the other person with whom you have conflict is someone you want to maintain a close connection with, there is a lot more at stake than whatever the immediate conflict is about. You have the whole history of your relationship and hopefully the future as well. The long-term health of the relationship, not to mention the good of the other person, is what is at stake.

When you can validate the other person, the objective shifts from proving your point to establishing deeper connection. If you both know that the other isn't just trying to prove a point, then you can trust each other to engage in a conversation that will lead to a deeper understanding of each other. You now have the shared goal of love despite the conflict. Rather than trying to win, you are both now playing the game to grow in intimacy.

"Do You Want to Be Right or Do You Want to Be Happy?"

Validity always precedes solutions. Some of us may view conflict as an opportunity for problem-solving. Problem-solving is okay, but I frequently see people skip the preliminary step of validating someone's perspective. Until we understand the other person's issues and concerns, finding a helpful solution will be much more challenging. Many times, people want to skip this step and jump straight to fixing things, but how can we fix what we don't understand?

When I think about validity, I often think about a quote from the famous TV psychologist Dr. Phil: "Do you want to be right or do you want to be happy?" Many people respond to that question by saying they want both. Unfortunately, if one of you wins an argument, that means the other person loses. And if one of you loses, the relationship loses.

At the end of the day, we must decide what's more important: winning or feeling connected. When we try to win, we might feel a temporary sense of satisfaction but we've left the door open for loneliness to creep into the relationship. On the other hand, when we prioritize closeness, we kick loneliness to the curb.

In conflict with friends, try to remember that it's usually not the other person's words that matter but rather their feelings. If you need to hear this, I give you permission to express sorrow that your friend is feeling hurt while still not apologizing for something you didn't do. English is limited with apologies, but saying "I'm sorry" doesn't have to mean "What I did was wrong." It can also mean "I can see you are in pain and I am saddened by how you feel." Even if a friend thinks you intentionally hurt them, acknowledging how somebody feels and affirming their experience does not mean that you agree with their interpretation of events. Step back, look at the big picture, and ask yourself what you really care about: being right, or what this person—created in the image and likeness of God—is experiencing?

Learning to Share, Learning to Listen

At the marriage preparation retreat mentioned at the beginning of the chapter, our presenter was trying to teach my husband and I the effectiveness of I-statements. Here's how it works, and see the model dialogue below for reference: The speaker makes a short, simple statement that begins with the word *I* and expresses their subjective emotions, experience, or feelings. The person making the I-statement is limited to describing how they feel without making a judgment of the other person. This helps the listener to just listen, as they are less likely to feel like they are being attacked. Consider how these two sentences would make you react and you will get the idea: "I feel frustrated when I clear the table alone" versus "You never clean the table!" Both might be true, but it's hard to dispute the first one because it only relates the interior reality of the speaker's experience. The second sentence leaves the door open for a verbal tennis match.

The listener's job is simply to mirror back the statement as they heard it without any judgment, interpretation, or spin. In other words, they are asked to seek full understanding and to approach the conversation with a disposition of curiosity. So, if my husband had said, "I feel sad when we don't get to talk about my day," my job would be to say, "What I hear you saying is, you feel hurt you don't get a chance to talk about your day." If I summarize sufficiently, my husband should feel understood and will let me know. Then I can ask him if there's any more to clarify or add. If I misunderstood or didn't summarize accurately, he repeats or clarifies his I-statement, and he does so until he feels understood.

This step is helpful to the speaker because when they hear the listener mirror their statement, it gives the speaker an opportunity to make sure they are conveying the message clearly. The speaker continues with simple I-statements until they have shared completely. If necessary, the listener then apologizes and takes their turn as the speaker, and on it goes. Both people share the power, which is one of the reasons why this is such a helpful technique. If each person commits to their role as speaker and listener out of love and respect for each other, that's when the magic happens.

Helpful I-statements	Hurtful statements
I feel frustrated when I have to clear the table by myself.	You are lazy and don't pick up your plate, so I have to.
I feel disrespected when it appears as if you are looking at your phone while I'm trying to share something important.	All you do is look at your phone; you don't care about what is important to me.
I would really feel so loved if you said hello to me when I got home from work.	You can't even bother to look up from watching TV when I walk in the house!

I don't appreciate when our private conversations are shared with your dad.	Your nosy dad needs to mind his business and stop interfering in our marriage.

Be Gentle with Each Other

Imagine you are peacefully reading a book on the couch. Your mother comes over to visit and before you even have a chance to say hello, she tears into you. "I can't believe you're just sitting there when your apartment looks like this. I'm so sick of coming over here to this mess. You're such a slob, and I'm always picking up after you." You look around the apartment to try to figure out what she's talking about. You notice a glass half full of water on the coffee table that you were just drinking out of and your backpack and shoes are still by the door from work. But it doesn't matter what your apartment looks like. When someone starts an argument like this, it's not going to end well.

It's normal to experience strong emotions in any conflict. You get an increase in adrenaline and your fight-flight-or-freeze response kicks in. When we feel attacked, our hearts race and we begin to feel everything from frustration to fury. But conflict doesn't have to be this way.

Leading marriage researcher Dr. John Gottman has discovered one of the biggest secrets to healthy conflict. Those who manage conflict well start and stay gentle throughout. Rather than launch into what upset them with accusations and a raised voice, skilled conflict navigators begin with a tone of tenderness, kindness, and respect. They enter the conversation with the bigger picture in mind and a desire to maintain and preserve the health of the relationship.

The opposite is true of those who start with criticism. Dr. Gottman's research found that criticism is one of the deadliest things to a relationship because it sows seeds of doubt that chip away at your relational bond. Starting with criticism is probably the fastest way to end a conflict without healthy resolution, as it is so likely to offend the other person and make them walk away in anger.

The next time you need to have a hard discussion with someone, I invite you to start it gently and without criticism. This is a respectful approach that lets somebody know that you would like to talk about a difficult topic and you're asking for their input about when to resolve the conflict. This is respectful for several reasons. You acknowledge the importance of the other person's time and respect their freedom to enter into the conversation or not. You also avoid making hurtful and inflammatory comments in a moment of anger—comments you are likely to regret later.

Here's what being gentle looks like. In the previous scenario, the mother could have started with "Hey son / daughter, I hope you're doing well today. There's something that's been on my mind that I'm hoping we can discuss. Is now a good time to talk? If not, we can always find another time that works for both of us." Now the power is in the other person's hands and they can decide if they're ready. If they are, great. The mother has already started off on the right foot, and that is key. Dr. Gottman's research into relationship dynamics reveals that most arguments end the way they begin. If you start a conflict respectfully, it is more likely to end respectfully. If you come in hot, guess how it's going to end?

How responsible are we for the way other people feel? It's easy to think of the extremes, but I think a reasonable person would understand that their words and actions have the potential to positively or negatively influence another person's happiness and well-being. After all, how many people don't appreciate recognition for a job well done? This is related to our interdependence, something that is part of the way God created us. In a mysterious way, we belong to one another and are our brother's keeper. Recent research sheds light on what this means for us with respect to interpersonal communication.

According to Christine Porath in her book *Mastering Civility: A Manifesto for the Workplace,* incivility or harshness in the workplace has negative consequences on people's health. Incivility in the workplace can lead to a shorter life span through increased risk of problems such as cardiovascular disease, cancer, and diabetes. It can also negatively impact memory, creativity, and overall mental health. Not surprisingly, people in uncivil organizations are less likely to put in the effort and time to accomplish key goals. If this is what incivility does at work, what do you think happens when it comes from those closest to us, the people we turn to for encouragement, affirmation, and affection?

What does this mean for our relationships? I interpret this to mean that when we are mindful of the other person's heart and soul while broaching a difficult topic, we can address difficulties and not only preserve our relationship but strengthen it as well! We're also much more likely to find a helpful solution. It seems that the opposite is also true. When we blame or criticize, erupt out of anger, and show disrespect, we roll out the red carpet for separation and distance. Unless we are willing to protect our conversations from beginning to end, and unless we are willing to take a close look at ourselves to ensure that happens, we won't find ourselves resolving conflict in a healthy way. As Christians, we are called to live virtuous lives, and that virtue can be present with how we approach our arguments as well.

Take Responsibility

The next key in managing conflict is taking responsibility. I witness a lot of disagreements in my line of work, and I can attest to the truth of the adage "It takes two to tango." At least, it's uncommon for one person to be completely culpable and the other person to be blameless. If you have a conflict with someone, there's a good chance that you did at least one thing imperfectly. This doesn't mean you're a bad person; it just means you made a mistake. We are sinful, imperfect people and we all make mistakes. But what makes followers of Jesus different is that we ask for forgiveness and resolve to do better. The saint is someone who got up one more time than they fell down.

If you are willing to take responsibility for your missteps, you'll enjoy higher-quality relationships. This means more emotional intimacy and less loneliness. So how do you take responsibility? If you are using I-statements to communicate and you realize that you did something wrong, try saying something like "I'm sorry. You're right. You have asked me to help keep our place clean, and I said I would. I'll do better. When you are ready, I ask for your forgiveness." It can also sound as simple as "I've been so stressed at work lately. I'm sorry I was short with you" or "I haven't been getting much sleep lately. I wish I was more present to you during our conversation."

Some things are easier to forgive than others, so be prepared for others to take a while to heal. While you wait, continue to do for your friend or loved one as you would want them to do for you. This is a form of taking responsibility and can facilitate healing as well. For instance, in the case of an affair, after apologizing, the offending spouse will need to demonstrate by deeds more than words that they are completely committed to their spouse. With every sacrifice or task done in love, they are building up the bridge of trust that they need to move forward.

It would be irresponsible of me not to point out that you can do all the right things and things may still not work out. You can use I-statements all day, start every conversation gently, be empathetic, and even bring someone cupcakes. If they aren't willing to meet you in the middle, that is beyond your control. The good news is that you are only responsible for you. Everyone has a bad day, and just because someone didn't respond well today doesn't mean it will be the same tomorrow. You can still rest your head knowing that you acted as God wanted you to. If you string a bunch of those days together, that will make for a good life.

Embracing Conflict

If you have been raised to think that conflict is a bad thing and that it should be avoided at all costs, I invite you to think of conflict differently. To have conflict in a relationship does not mean that something is going wrong. This couldn't be farther from the truth!

Conflict, when healthy, is good for relationships because it binds people closer together. Again, it might seem a bit voyeuristic, but as a relationship therapist, I look forward to helping people work through their conflict. I don't get enjoyment out of their frustration; rather, I know what lies on the other side if they're willing to wade into the discomfort. They are headed toward much greater intimacy and connection, and that makes the conflict worth it.

If you have the eyes to see, conflict can be a portal to emotional intimacy. With these new tools I hope you can view conflict as an opportunity to grow closer to and strengthen your connection with everyone in your life. I invite you to embrace the discomfort the next time you encounter conflict. When you do, I hope you stay curious, listen for meaning, validate people, and stay gentle. If you're willing to brave the dangers of potentially hurtful words with charity in your mind and love as the goal, you can arrive at a deeper, more fulfilling connection. You simply must be willing to do the hard work of communicating well to get there. Be not afraid.

4

The Layers
Our Past Wounds and Seeking Healing

> I have found the paradox, that if you love until it hurts, there can be no more hurt, only more love.
> —St. Mother Teresa of Calcutta

> In my deepest wound I saw your glory and it dazzled me.
> —St. Augustine of Hippo

Sometimes we can do everything right. We try to be kind and loving, caring and nurturing. We encourage our loved ones in their faith and even make sure our relationships are rooted in the love of Jesus. We extend ourselves, become vulnerable, and yet we still experience loneliness. Why is that?

One of the most common reasons you might still experience loneliness, despite your best efforts, is that you've been hurt. But this isn't just any type of hurt. This is the worst type. Someone you loved, respected, or were close to and who should have treated you with dignity, did not. You were betrayed. This doesn't come from strangers, for they don't owe you what a friend, relative, or loved one owes you. You can only be betrayed by someone you love. When this happens, the vital balance of trust that is necessary for connection and relationship is damaged.

When we are betrayed, we might find it difficult and in some cases even impossible to connect with others. One of the reasons this is so challenging and hard to move past is that it's not our fault. No one deserves to be betrayed, and yet the impact can be catastrophic. It simply feels unjust that we should be the ones who are unable to connect and experience intimacy because of what someone else did. Afterall, they are the offender in this situation. They are the one who created the distance between us.

Unfortunately I don't have a great answer for you. You are right; it's not your fault. It's not fair that it's difficult to connect with others because of something that happened to you. It just isn't. And yet acknowledging that without moving forward will only leave us lonely. I wish I had a better answer than that, but I don't. However, I know how to help you move forward. Please, for your happiness, embrace the process of healing. That's what this chapter is about.

A Heartbreaking Betrayal

A woman came to my office once and I could see she was worried to her core. She nervously entered the room and sat cautiously and stiffly on the couch, fidgeting with her purse handle. She introduced herself as Lily. Her gaunt face told me that she probably hadn't been sleeping or eating much. She just learned that her husband of twenty years had been unfaithful to her. Lily cried and visibly shook as she shared the story about how she discovered his infidelity. It was not a one-night encounter. This was a long-term relationship, and her husband had grown very attached to this other person. Lily was heartbroken. Her mind and her story went in so many different directions while she was sharing, it was as if she were piecing together shattered glass. After explaining everything that had happened, Lily—still in a state of shock—paused, grabbed a tissue to wipe her eyes, and looked at me. "Can anyone come back from this?"

I've been asked this question many times. People often want to know if their marriage can be saved. Can they be healed? Is their situation "too crazy," too big of a betrayal? Should they just cut their losses now?

While it is true that some of the most painful wounds come from people we love, the good news is that you can be healed. The same God who created you for intimacy and connection, who died on the Cross to save you, also created you to be able to recover, heal, and grow. Jesus desires to heal and transform your past wounds. Know this: healing is not far off! In this chapter we are going to explore why betrayal is so destructive, how to recognize its signs, and how to feel free to connect deeply with others.

Psychological Impact of Betrayal

To better understand how to find your way out of this painful maze, let's talk about what's happening psychologically when you are betrayed. Betrayal is a violation of trust, and it can shake you to the very core. The effects of betrayal include shock, loss and grief, morbid preoccupation, damaged self-esteem, self-doubt, and anger. Not infrequently, betrayal produces life-altering changes. Catastrophic betrayal can even result in post-traumatic stress disorder (PTSD). It ultimately causes real harm because it's a disruption of certainty within that relationship. Being able to have confidence in someone is what makes your relationship worthwhile. Trust represents the confidence you have in another person. It reflects how dependable someone is in your life, how much you can depend upon them. When you trust, you can explore the depths of connection and friendship with emotional safety. Mature, durable relationships such as what you experience in family, friendships, and marriage enjoy levels of trust that create the sense of belonging that we all crave.

Assurance about someone's character grows out of the countless and seemingly trivial interactions that occur over time. This is why there is no substitute for time in establishing deep friendships. Why do you think your best friends are often ones you met in high school, college, or young adulthood when you had time to waste?

When your interactions with someone are net positive, they collectively convey trustworthiness about the other. When you share a personal story or an embarrassing moment, you get to experience another person affirming your dignity. When you expose your heart and the other person responds with respect and compassion, you know it's safe to be yourself and it paves the way for the other person to reciprocate and share more of themselves as well. When a person keeps your secrets without betraying you, or when someone is present in times of need, they communicate that they are trustworthy, that your relationship is one you can count on. Moments like these are what contribute to an overall sense of dependability in a relationship. Trust is what allows you to feel at home and be yourself with another person.

When that kind of trust is broken, we are thrown into a disorienting chaos. The emotions and psychological effects associated with betrayal are extensive: uncertainty, confusion, fear, anger, pain, sadness, fatigue, and ruminating thoughts. You might start replaying conversations in your head or feel as if the rug has been pulled out from under you. Some people report mental contamination, or feelings of dirtiness, shame, or guilt that can arise after an experience of betrayal. While those close to us are most often the culprit, we can even feel rejected by things such as our culture, our country, or even our own body after a bout with illness or serious injury.

When you lose trust, your relationship is weakened. You are less likely to risk vulnerability, and as a result, the pathways to emotional intimacy are inhibited. Even if you might want to be vulnerable, your body will likely have built up psychological armor to protect you, preventing you from exposing yourself to further harm. Protecting your susceptible emotions is a natural reaction to betrayal.

Betrayal and Trauma

There isn't complete agreement on this in the mental health field yet, but as we become more informed about the intricacies of trauma, more and more people are starting to see that betrayal is a form of trauma. This is probably why many people who experience betrayal display symptoms associated with PTSD. This is especially true for infidelity, infertility (being betrayed by your body), and other serious deceptions.

I believe there are many people walking around carrying the weight of trauma without realizing it. Our culture values pushing forward, moving on, and working at any cost. We often don't have time to slow down and perceive when we're hurting. We also undervalue rest and healing because it is perceived by our culture as unproductive. For those who do have the luxury of taking time to heal, talking about the need to heal and asking for help is still a cultural taboo. This may be changing as people recognize the importance of mental and emotional wellbeing, but the stigma is still enough of a barrier to keep people from speaking openly.

Even if you don't believe you've experienced PTSD symptoms, the effects of betrayal are serious and deserve to be addressed. I want you to be able to recognize the signs of PTSD, not only for yourself but for anyone close to you whom you may be able to encourage to seek help.

When I think back to Lily and her situation, she presented several symptoms consistent with PTSD. She reported restlessness, irritability, disturbed sleep, and hypervigilance whenever her husband would leave the house. She became highly concerned about all the details of his comings and goings and felt compelled to check his emails, messages, and GPS location. Often it would feel like a million questions, scenarios, and images were flashing through her mind with so much force that she couldn't ignore them.

These are common PTSD responses to infidelity. When you hear the term *PTSD*, you might think of a war veteran or victim of violent crime. To be sure, those are groups who frequently experience the horrific effects of PTSD. Like the combat veteran, someone who has been betrayed is in survival mode, feeling as if their life could be at risk at any moment. When a core need like safety, shelter, and belonging is in flux, this type of chronic stress is what can lead to PTSD.

For Lily, the sense of safety in her relationship was destroyed and she was left questioning if anything in life was actually safe. The man she had trusted with her heart had betrayed her. If she couldn't trust him, what could she trust? Lily was exposed to the trauma of feeling unsafe in her entire environment. She was in a constant state of unrest, and it doesn't take long before that has debilitating effects.

Attachment and Trust

Attachment theory was created by the psychologist John Bowlby. He studied childhood development and theorized that a child's relationship with their caregivers would influence how the child would attach or relate to others throughout life, for better and for worse. The influence of attachment styles is due to our need for belonging. We are social beings created for communion with one another. Bowlby knew this and found that when caretakers were not sufficiently loving or nurturing to young children, it negatively shaped the way those children formed relationships as adults. He found that some may grow into adults who have difficulty trusting others, establishing healthy boundaries and interdependencies, or feeling confidence in any type of relationship. They could be people who wonder if others are truly their friends, who long to share more deeply but don't know how, or those who indiscriminately show vulnerability to others, including those who may hurt them. We now know that it is not only our childhood experiences that influence or create ways of relating to others. Our adult experiences can also influence how we interact. In Amir Levine and Rachel S. F. Heller's book *Attached*, the authors bring to light new research which suggests a combination of sources for our attachment styles including evolutionary development, child-rearing, and adult interactions.

They and Bowlby identified four types of attachment styles in their research: anxious, avoidant, ambivalent, and secure.

Anxious Attachment Style

Someone who relates with an anxious attachment style may have had parents who were emotionally unavailable or inconsistent when, as a child, they expressed legitimate needs. Or they may have experienced an early separation from their caregivers. Both the potential for neglect and the experience of separation can send a message to the child that they are not valuable or wanted.

An anxious attachment style in adults manifests in behaviors such as worrying about the security of their relationships. They strongly crave intimacy. Adults relating with this attachment style may wonder if the other person is as invested as they are and if the other person has the ability to reciprocate equal emotions. They may do things like call or text multiple times after receiving no response. These adults may also tend to hold others in high regard while thinking very little of the value they bring to relationships.

Have you ever known people who spoke negatively about themselves and the value they bring their relationship with you while simultaneously praising and thanking you for what you do with them? This may be an expression of an anxious attachment style. In adolescents, this may manifest as a dependency on others or as a need to be reassured of the stability of the relationship. This could be seen in asking to speak, text, or meet in person with a higher frequency than the other person in the relationship feels comfortable with. While recognizing its limitations, the stereotype here would be the teenager who is constantly draped across the shoulder of their significant other, can't find time for anything or anyone else, and finds it difficult to find meaning on his or her own. This anxiousness can also affect someone's relationship with God. Adults experiencing anxious attachment styles may wonder how they could ever be lovable enough to God. They might also feel a strong compulsion to follow rules and obey in order to receive love and affection. This can lead to an internal pressure to be perfectionistic or feeling the need to fit a mold to be worthy of God's love.

Avoidant Attachment Style

A person who develops an avoidant attachment style may have experienced caregivers who discouraged the expression of feelings or were emotionally distant or rigid. They may have been raised with values of independence and strength. This seeking of independence might have gone to an extreme where maintaining relationships became challenging. Someone who relates with an avoidant attachment becomes very distant in their relationships. They avoid intimate moments out of concern of being smothered, hurt, or overwhelmed based on their past experiences of emotional distance or unresponsiveness. Though they deeply desire intimacy and connection, they fear that intimacy leads to a loss of their independence.

The social stereotypes that may be influenced by this attachment style include both the workaholic and someone who engages in a series of casual relationships, especially of a sexual nature. In both scenarios, the result is that people avoid relationship commitments. For the workaholic, he or she can use the excuse of work demands as an easy way out of dedicating the time a relationship needs to grow.

For those who create a long string of shallow relationships, including sexual ones, it might seem counter-intuitive that such a person would have difficulty with attachment. They make friends and connect with people easily, right? Afterall, they desire intimacy as well. The reality is that it's challenging to develop deep connections as they move on from one relationship to the next before the time in which it's practically expected or required to be more vulnerable and forthcoming. The television caricature of this person could be the successful, wealthy lawyer or business leader who is also a womanizer, who also can't comfortably share his feelings. Often, this attachment style can be seen as strength of character, as someone might pride themselves on being hardworking or perhaps guarded in close friendships. They appear to be clear, direct, level-headed and detached, which conveys leadership. Of course, the truth is that moderation in both work ethic and interpersonal vulnerability lies in the middle of two extremes.

In their relationship with God, a person experiencing avoidant attachment can fear deep intimacy with God. They may view their relationship with God as strictly a rule-book type of relationship rather than deep personal sharing or being a part of God's family. For those with an avoidant style, it may be more comfortable to do the work God asks in regard to serving others rather than to have a deeply personal, intimate prayer life. In the story of the prodigal son in Luke 15, the older brother exhibits behavior that could be interpreted as avoidant attachment. "Look, all these years I served you and not once did I disobey your orders; yet you never gave me even a young goat to feast on with my friends" (Lk 15:29).

Ambivalent Attachment Style

Ambivalent attachment styles are born out of situations of abuse or neglect when a child experiences both ends of the attachment spectrum. The pendulum swings back and forth from moments of unsafety and fear to moments of love and apology. These children can grow into adults who are confused about who they can trust because their caregivers did not model trust through a safe and stable environment. In adult relationships, people with an ambivalent attachment style can show a strong desire for intimacy one moment and then push you away in the next. They may vacillate between strong emotions and be slow to trust. This makes a relationship with God challenging. Putting all their confidence in a God who is supposed to love them, care for them, and provide for them creates a sense of discomfort because of their childhood experiences of abuse or neglect. Their caregivers indirectly taught them that God is undependable, subject to wild mood swings, and just as likely to show love as to show wrath.

This style of attachment proves to be effective for many children who learn to survive and adapt while exposed to unreliable or unstable home environments. Whether it is physical or emotional abuse or neglect experienced, the ability to adapt is incredibly useful in that it helps children be more prepared for an outburst of anger or a moment of unsafety. However, sometimes these skills don't always transfer well into adult relationships. The ambivalent attachment style can influence some to be "hot" one minute and "cold" the next. This can be confusing to those who are friends with or dating someone with an ambivalent attachment style as they are unsure where they stand in the relationship and may feel unsure about their ability to trust that individual's true feelings.

Secure Attachment Style

Lastly is secure attachment; happily, most people fall into this category. A secure attachment develops when one's caregivers are sufficiently responsive to physical, mental, and emotional needs such that the child learns that the world is a safe, good place and that others can be trusted. As adults, these individuals can engage in deep intimacy without fear of being smothered and enjoy independence without fear of abandonment or vengeance. As you can imagine, this would impact one's relationship with God positively as well. People with secure attachment styles are more likely to trust that God will provide for their needs and that it is safe to trust him. They are more likely to have moments of spiritual intimacy and closeness that do not create a fear response.

By now, you may have tried to identify your attachment style. If you think that you have an unhealthy attachment style, you might feel a little unsettled. Have no fear! This is not intended to be a clinical diagnosis, nor is it permanent. People's attachment styles can change. In fact, one recent study by Hudson, Chopkin, and Briley found that simply identifying one's attachment style can be enough to help develop a more secure attachment, if they desire to do so. We also know that attachment styles change to be more secure as a person experiences healthy interactions with others, even in adulthood. Reading this book means you are looking for healing, and the Lord will honor your seeking. You are on your way to building healthy connections.

Now would be a good time to turn to the workbook to think more about your own attachment style and identify what could be added in order to increase experiences of a more secure attachment style. You can also reflect on what might have been missing from the way you interacted with your early caregivers.

How to Heal

I've helped many people rebuild trust, both in their relationships and trust with themselves. I've witnessed people experience freedom after being deeply hurt. Being aware of your attachment style is one way to identify ways you've been wounded in the past. This awareness provides insight into what areas of your heart might desire restoration. Here are four ways you can develop a more secure attachment style so that you can have more confidence in your relationships and in yourself. I recommend that you start by choosing just one of these four and commit to implementing this into your life for the next week or month.

Four Life-Giving Remedies

Baby Steps

Rebuilding trust takes time, and it's okay to take small steps. This is especially true in cases of abuse, assault, or neglect. It may also be unsafe to rebuild trust with someone who is violent or puts your safety in jeopardy. I'm giving you permission not to do so until you are completely ready and confident in your safety.

I've spoken with many people who become frustrated when they aren't "getting over it by now." Sometimes we place arbitrary deadlines on ourselves in regard to when we think we should be feeling better. That is an unnecessary layer of pressure to put on yourself. If you notice that a hurt is staying with you longer than you would like, I believe this is because the impact could be more than just hurt feelings. Like we discussed earlier, trauma is a completely different category. If you suspect you are dealing with trauma, I highly recommend you find a therapist you connect with and continue your journey of healing with a professional.

In Lily's case, she was undecided for several months if she wanted to continue her relationship with her husband. They continued to live together, but they were very emotionally distant and separate, only communicating about the children and household responsibilities. Once she decided that she was ready to try to reconcile with her husband, it took even more time in counseling and working together as a couple before she was able to trust him again. What was the hardest of all was being willing to reengage in a sexual relationship with her husband after the affair. He thought sex represented healing and moving forward, but she was particularly concerned about a sexually transmitted disease (STD) and their physical relationship was a trigger for her. One baby step toward rekindling trust was for her husband to agree to get tested on a regular basis until they could be sure he didn't have an STD. After that, intimacy needed to progress very gradually, almost as if they were dating for the first time again.

When you've experienced betrayal, taking baby steps can look like praying for the person who hurt you; saying out loud, "I forgive you" (either alone or to them); sending a text message or letter to explain how their choice impacted you; or even meeting for coffee in an attempt to begin reconciling. Whatever steps you take, you have full permission to take your time and go at a pace that is comfortable for you.

Boundaries

Remembering to maintain appropriate boundaries is important. As long as you can still fulfill your state in life, it's okay to set boundaries! If someone has repeatedly shown disregard for you and your feelings, it's okay to decide not to be in their physical presence or to limit your conversation to text only rather than by phone. Boundaries help you to preserve your integrity and sanity.

It's also okay to speak up for yourself and protect yourself from getting hurt. Just because this person has hurt you does not mean you are defenseless in their presence. You can tell them how they have caused you pain in the past and ask them not to do it again, giving them an opportunity to amend and change their behavior. It also helps them understand your expectations for a new, healthy relationship with you moving forward. Lily felt the need to discuss the emotional impact her husband's infidelity had on her, and she also expressed concern about some of his friends. This was especially true of those friends who were aware of his infidelity and did nothing to dissuade him at the time. This was a boundary she needed to feel comfortable moving forward and seeking reconciliation. Not everyone will receive a boundary well, and that is okay. Take comfort knowing that you took steps toward healing and it will take time for some to adjust and find a new way forward. In the meantime, you can pray for them until they are ready.

Forgiveness

Forgiveness is a big ask, but hear me out and allow me to put a few caveats here. Forgiving someone does not mean that the relationship is magically restored. It certainly does not mean you put your safety in jeopardy by being in the presence of someone who could harm you. It also does not mean you are saying that what happened was okay or that the other person wasn't wrong.

Forgiveness is a process with multiple stages. One of the first stages is just to give yourself freedom from the pain. Jesus teaches us to be merciful as God is merciful. He also challenges us to forgive so that we can be rescued from our own pain. In Matthew 18:21–22 Peter asks Jesus, "'Lord, if my brother sins against me, how often must I forgive him? As many as seven times?' Jesus answered, 'I say to you, not seven times but seventy-seven times.'" I love this quote from the theologian Lewis B. Smedes: "To forgive is to set a prisoner free and discover that the prisoner was you." Even if you must do it seventy-seven times, you will find it was worth it to be set free.

Now, here comes one of the more challenging stages. Full healing means that we forgive the people who hurt us. Why? The most straightforward answer is that Jesus asks us to extend forgiveness to others *so that we can be forgiven*. We aren't living as God intended us to live until we forgive as he forgives. This idea is right there in the Our Father: "Forgive us our trespasses as we forgive those who trespass against us." The importance of forgiveness is also painfully visible in the parable of the unforgiving servant (Mt 18:21–35). Forgiveness is just one of the things that we do as Christians. Now for the really hard part . . . not everyone asks for forgiveness. And yet Jesus even forgave us before we ever asked for absolution. "But God proves his love for us in that while we were still sinners Christ died for us" (Rom 5:8).

Forgiveness is a courageous act of deep love. Try to imagine or visualize being a channel of God's love, bestowing that love on others in the world. Imagine being on the other side of Jesus's Cross, with arms outstretched, in pain on behalf of others. That is what forgiveness looks like. It's messy and agonizing, but forgiveness brings redemptive healing to the world (Col 1:24, "Now I rejoice in my sufferings for your sake . . . I am filling up what is lacking in the afflictions of Christ"). When you coura- geously take that step toward mercy, you are not only bound up in Jesus's ultimate act of forgiveness but you are also freeing yourself from the pain that you may be holding on to from the wrong committed. Again, forgiveness does not mean you now have to have a relationship with this person, that everything is reconciled, or that you must pretend as if nothing ever happened. But forgiveness can be an act of the heart that provides a healing balm to emotional wounds—yours and theirs.

While you're at it, don't forget to forgive yourself. Guilt and shame often creep in after a betrayal. We can blame ourselves for putting ourselves in a position to be taken advantage of or wonder why we didn't see it coming. We might even feel ashamed for being angry at the injustice of the circumstances. But we must extend mercy and compassion to ourselves. When you are involved in a stressful situation, you might respond in ways that are not typical for you. Be patient with yourself in those moments. This betrayal was not your fault! It was the result of another person's actions or perhaps the result of a health condition beyond your control. Don't allow mental contamination to creep in and distort the truth about who you really are—a beloved child of God.

After some encouragement, Lily practiced extending grace to herself. It was tempting to think about all the things that went wrong in her marriage before her husband's affair. She recounted the times she was short or unkind and how they let the busyness of life get in between them. Even though these issues needed to be addressed, she still didn't deserve the shame, guilt, and negativity that bubbled up as a result of her sense of mental contamination. To find reprieve and healing, Lily needed to be compassionate toward herself. This meant attempting to heal without judging herself severely for her husband's infidelity, even though she hadn't been the perfect wife.

I will add that forgiveness does not have to look like a face-to-face meeting with the betrayer. You can journal about your decision to forgive, adding language that you might use if you were in their presence. Perhaps prayerfully saying the words to the person aloud as if they were in the room with you could be an exercise in healing and steps toward forgiveness.

I'm sure you've seen by now that the process of forgiveness and healing is not straight or sequential, and that's okay! Even when you feel like you've put something in the past, new feelings might surface and surprise you. This does not mean that you have not grown, changed, or healed. Rather, it is a new invitation toward even deeper healing and wholeness. When these moments pop up, know that you have the strength and the wisdom to respond to the Lord's call for you.

Address the Wounds

Ultimately we must face that which is painful to us. There's a saying that I really love: "The only way to, is through." After all, there is no Resurrection without the Cross. To get to the other side of our pain, we have to first acknowledge our hurt and confront our crosses head-on. Our wounds are real and not to be ignored, hidden, or suppressed. You are worthy of healing, and you deserve to have a moment where you are validated through your encounters with others.

To get there, we must acknowledge that we've been hurt. Without that acknowledgment, it is impossible to find healing. In scripture, we see Jesus ask people if they want to be healed before he performs the miracle, and it is only the sick who need a physician (Mk 2:17). We cannot receive freedom from struggle without recognizing that past events have left us scarred. Acknowledging how we have been hurt can demand heroic vulnerability for some. However, there is freedom on the other side for those who venture forth.

Now that I've hopefully convinced you to acknowledge your pain, it is helpful to take time discerning when to address it. Though we may be able to identify a pain point, that does not mean that it is time or that we are emotionally ready to address the issue. It would be helpful to discern how to address each wound, recognizing that it could look different for each situation. You may be able to easily set aside memories of teasing in middle school, but you may need a more intricate plan to address the pain of a chronic illness. In the previous chapter, we discussed some communication strategies that can help you have a conversation about your past in a safe way. One of the steps is to make sure that when you share with someone, they are ready to engage in a deep exchange with you. I recommend you do the same here.

This is exactly what Lily did with her husband. She took baby steps and set appropriate boundaries. Together they created a plan that would help her feel comfortable and secure in their relationship, and it included things like checking in frequently to let her know about his location. These were the boundaries she needed to feel safe and comfortable moving forward. Over time, these check-ins became less necessary and less frequent as their trust began to grow.

They also had to address the elephant in the room and talk about his infidelity. This was an important conversation that needed structure and guidelines. We created an environment where it was safe for Lily to ask her husband questions. For example, "When you said you had to work late that one night, were you really going to see her?" He would then answer openly and honestly, and there were many moments of tears, anger, and emotion. However, it was an integral step toward finding healing and rebuilding the trust between them. To build a new relationship together, he was going to have to be honest with Lily about all his past relationships, including the infidelity. But we were mindful to avoid specific details about sexual encounters so as not to cause any more trauma.

As you can imagine, this was a grueling process. Lily's husband had to apologize and take responsibility ad nauseum. He sometimes found himself repeating apologies as painful memories resurfaced for Lily, and she had to be brave enough to bring them to his attention, trusting that he would honor her vulnerability. This is what acknowledging betrayal is like. It's neither pretty nor easy. It certainly is not orderly, nor does it happen in a linear fashion. However, every time Lily acknowledged that pain and brought it to her husband, and every time he responded with a genuine apology, they added a brick of trust to the new foundation of their relationship. As they rebuilt the foundation, they began to see a light on the horizon and eventually learned to relax in each other's presence again. They also acknowledged what it was in their relationship that led to their past emotional distance. Lily acknowledged her shortcomings, how the way she had treated him led her husband to seek affirmation and intimacy from another. When she took ownership, that encouraged her husband to do the same.

After months of deep, emotionally taxing work, they found themselves in love all over again, experiencing a deeper connection than they had ever previously enjoyed. Though the wounds from the past are still there, they hold much less power over Lily and her husband now. By embracing the healing process, they found a new freedom and learned to trust and, more importantly, to forgive.

5

The Gift

Self-Donation

Whoever loses his life for my sake will find it.
—Matthew 16:25

I've asked you to travel into the deep parts of your heart and address issues that have been holding you back from emotional intimacy. I'm confident that you have found some keys to open doors to new and fulfilling authentic connection. For others, perhaps you already knew how to handle conflict, communication, vulnerability, and healing. Maybe you didn't have a deep desire to strengthen your relationships because they were already strong. Whichever group you belong to, I'd wager that there is still something about some or even all your relationships that still nags you. It's there, like a little rock in your shoe, telling you that you can find more in your relationships. In some small, perhaps almost imperceptible way, do you still feel a whisper of loneliness?

The problem is that loneliness can exist even if you know how to be vulnerable, communicate your needs, and forgive others, and you've experienced healing. In part, this is because we were made for union with God in heaven, and nothing on earth can fully satisfy us. But loneliness exists because we have not fully embraced the truth of who we are and what we were made for. We can all find more ways to make a gift of life to others. We are imperfect. We experience the effects of our sin and the sin of everyone around us, and this poses a challenge to authentic, selfless love. So what are we to do about this?

"Learn from Me . . . and You Will Find Rest for Yourselves."–Matthew 11:29

Throughout this book I have made the case that being open to others and making a gift of yourself is the way to life and relationships as God intended, and you probably agree with most of this. It is both intuitive and part of our cultural narrative that putting other people first is considered good. That aspect of Christianity has soaked into our culture, and it is now normal to think of others in that way.

But what about the ways Christianity hasn't yet soaked into our culture? Have we allowed the message of the Gospel to change the way we do everything, individually and collectively? The answer is probably no. We know we aren't perfect and yet Jesus invites us to pursue perfection, becoming more and more like him. This includes how we make a gift of ourselves to others.

Here is the main problem we face: we are called to a life of self-gift. The promise of happiness that comes from living this way is both believable and alluring. We are taught that if we learn to love like Jesus, we will experience relationships and connection as God intended. We are mostly okay with this when that self-gift stays within the bounds of the accepted cultural norms, our social script. If we want to be a self-sacrificing parent who puts the needs of our family first, society will affirm us for that, even if our sacrifices aren't always acknowledged.

But what if you want to do something more extreme? What if you want to extend the gift of yourself by living in solidarity with those who are poor? What if you want to avoid the use of questionable labor practices or try not to support organizations that work in ways contrary to the Gospel? You may be ridiculed or shunned, and people may accuse you of trying to live unrealistically. "Yeah, I could go without such and such, but the convenience of it and the way of modern society makes it just too hard to do otherwise." Can we imagine Jesus taking that approach? Want to forgive those who have grievously offended you or others? You might be told, "It's okay to forgive but not to forget." Would Jesus ever have uttered such a phrase?

A life of self-gift deviates from the social script and that is part of why it is so difficult. We need look no further than the life of Jesus. He stood out by being present, available to, and signaling the dignity of others. So too, if we stand out, we will experience some form of rejection. The perennial crossroad of life is one where the path of comfort runs across the path of meaning, connection, and selflessness. In writing these words, the choice seems easy, but it almost never is. And yet we still know that we want to choose the way of meaning, connection, and sacrifice.

In a terrible yet amusing way, self-gift is both the problem and the solution. It is the problem because it is so difficult. Selfishness is a way of life that we can slowly slide into until we find ourselves unsatisfied and lonely, even in close relationships. But self-gift is the solution because almost as fast as we start to think of other people, we find that our dissatisfaction dissipates and our loneliness gives way to connection. Making a gift of yourself is the final and vital key toward achieving emotional intimacy.

My family is tremendously blessed to have a community of families that frequently gather together. We play and pray together and encourage one another in life and in our marriages. At one gathering, one husband shared that he has a mental trick to help him be less selfish. Like with every couple, there are competing desires and sometimes they are mutually exclusive. For example both people can't get up early to workout and sleep in at the same time. He wishes they could, but he knows that wish won't come true. So when their conversations turn into a challenge of egos, he tries to remind himself that his job is not to look after his own interests, but rather to look after his wife's.

At the altar, they vowed to love each other and Christian love means making a gift of yourself to the other. It is easy to think, "But what about my needs—what about what I want? If I don't speak up for myself, who will?" And yet, my friend argues this line of thinking is a trap. Both he and his wife can always justify doing more for their individual selves, but they made a promise not to be a me-first person. One way he combats those temptations to be self-serving is by reminding himself of his wife's love for him and recalling that she will take care of him. This helps him be free to think of her, to love her, and to sacrifice what is important to him so that she can know God's sacrificial love through him. It's a pretty sweet deal.

To this day, he says that he has never gone wrong in choosing to love her and set his own concerns aside, even though it is often difficult and sometimes painful. If you are concerned this will turn someone into a human doormat, be at peace. I'm not recommending you should consent to anything that demeans your dignity, is sinful for you or the other person, or makes you feel unreasonably uncomfortable.

Imagine the possibilities if we lived our relationships with this pattern of trust and mutual love! Naturally, how we extend ourselves depends upon the type of relationship. Even in relationships where you won't have exchanged vows, the model of love that Jesus gave us on the Cross still informs how we establish intimacy with others.

Essentially, I am inviting you to say something like this to yourself: "I will put this person and their needs first. I trust that he or she is my friend and will also think of me, and I know that to the extent I depend upon him or her, my needs will be met." Tough as it may seem, we can still do this and act with prudence and wisdom, giving priority to our state in life, our spouse, children, family, and friends and always seeking to follow Jesus and fulfill our vocation.

In the short-term, this is difficult because it requires immediate sacrifice of something that seems urgent or important to us. We are left with a lingering fear of whether the other person will live up to our expectations for them. But in the long run, we begin to see who is really a friend, who has our best interest in mind and who is willing to also make sacrifices for us. And we see that loneliness diminishes whenever someone rises to the occasion.

Learning to Live Differently

I am a mental health counselor and marriage and family therapist, so not a day goes by when I don't work with someone who wants to learn to be a gift to others. They might not use these words, but that is what they are trying to accomplish. In this chapter, we are going to explore ordinary ways of allowing God to make extraordinary changes in your ability to be a gift to others. This will come by learning to recognize where you still have room to grow as well as how to find the opportunities for deep love, sacrifice, and connection that are right in front of you. To illustrate this, I'll start with a story of someone who had to take a similar journey.

I once knew a single parent whose life was a story of trying to allow the teachings of Jesus to transform her way of life more and more completely, but it didn't start that way. We will call her Nora. Her relationship with Anthony, the father of her three children, was extremely strained. They had never married, and Anthony was not involved in his children's lives. He would visit a couple of times each year and send child support just as infrequently. In so many ways, this made life hard.

In the early years as a mom, Nora always felt exhausted and torn between her kids and her dreams. When she and I started working together, Nora would share her dreams of meeting someone new and her desires to be taken care of, to have a partner and protector, and for her children to have a consistent male example.

The problem was that the more she thought about pursuing this goal, the more she tended to ignore her responsibilities. When her children were still small, Nora followed the social narrative of achieving her dream at any cost. She would stay out late, socializing with friends in the hopes that she would meet someone. She began casually dating men in the hopes of finding a husband. The trouble was that she settled for any man who paid her attention. If they entered into a sexual relationship, she justified it by convincing herself that it was a step on the way to a long-term commitment. However, man after man showed that they had no intention of marrying Nora and raising her children. They just wanted a cheap thrill. Day by day, her dream life seemed further and further away.

Nora began spending more nights away from home and asking her friends and family to stay with her children. The drinking, staying up late, and emotional turmoil that thrives in a hookup culture started to take its toll at home and work. After she ran out of excuses for being late to work, tired, and her emotional outbursts, she eventually lost her job. This was a wake-up call for Nora. As we discussed this event, she was finally able to take a step back, survey her life, and realize that she was pretty much at rock bottom. Her desire to seek her own happiness, which is valid when in balance and relationship to other responsibilities, had pulled her far away from the people and things she valued most.

As we explored the turn of events that had led Nora to this point, she realized that she was more invested in finding a new man than she was in her children. She had always made sure they were safe, secure, and cared for, but she wasn't giving them the best of herself. She had made an idol out of the dream of a husband, and this had caused her to become self-centered in not-so-subtle ways.

As we continued to discuss where she was, she shared that her older kids had begun to resent how much time she spent away from them. They were also forming closer attachments with the family and friends who cared for them. This was a huge red flag for Nora, as she had always dreamed of being the type of parent who was there for her kids when they needed her most. Now she had become the parent whose children went to others with their questions and concerns about life. She didn't want them to see her as unreliable and emotionally unavailable, but they did. She didn't want to be another adult who abandoned them, like their father. It was in this moment that Nora sensed a call to live differently.

This changed the tone of our meetings. Nora was beginning to respond to God's promptings to give more by looking for ways, both easy and challenging, to be a gift to her children. The low-hanging fruit, even though it was emotionally challenging, was to stop going out and meeting men. She had serious FOMO (fear of missing out) when she knew her friends were out meeting guys, but over time, and especially as she reestablished connection with her children, she cared less and less about what she thought she was missing out on. As time went on, she realized that God was asking her, at least temporarily, to live a chaste and almost consecrated life for the sake of her children and those closest to her.

At first, this thought left Nora feeling sad and empty. But as she leaned in to finding new ways to live a life of self-gift, she found that it was her lifestyle of intentional virginity that allowed her to be there for others so fully. Rather than a burden, she started to view it as a blessing.

Some of the more difficult steps included learning how to connect with her oldest child—a son who reminded her too much of Anthony and with whom she had always had a hard time connecting. Together we worked through ways to understand how he liked to spend time, how he communicated, and what was a normal relationship for a mother and son. As their relationship improved, Nora realized once again how it was her radical availability to her son that had made that relationship possible.

Learning to Give When It Isn't Easy

Within the sacred space of my office, I have seen what happens when people, especially couples, decide to act selflessly. It never goes wrong! Time and time again I've seen people start to experience more love, affection, connection, appreciation, and satisfaction, and all because they were willing to put their egos aside and choose to love first. Even something as simple as choosing to give someone the benefit of the doubt rather than judge harshly can be the difference between peace and war. Those small sacrifices coalesce over time to keep your relationships intact, preserving and protecting them from harm. Now, consider the times that you have not taken the higher road. How often did it lead to woundedness, distance, and mistrust?

If we are going to allow the love of God to transform us and the way we live, we can start by making a priority of authentic connection and emotional intimacy. This is countercultural because it means that we choose to sacrifice our egos and place Jesus at the center of our lives instead of ourselves. It means we make meaningful relationships with our life's work, we practice self-gift intentionally, and we never give up on it. In doing so, our lives will reveal the truth of who God is and what his love means for the world.

Discerning Your Path

The first step to discerning your path is to recognize that while we are all called to grow, not everyone has the same path. You and I have different struggles, and the way I need to embrace self-gift is different from the way you may need to. You might forgive easily but have a bad temper; I might rarely get upset but also struggle to forgive. We are both challenged by Jesus to be transformed by love, but we are yet unfinished masterpieces in different ways.

What is a practical way to learn how God is inviting you to challenge the social script? There is probably no better place to turn than the words of Jesus in the gospels. If you aren't too familiar with them, try looking up some famous parables or your favorite ones. I recommend going through the Sermon on the Mount in Matthew, chapters 5–7. In the corresponding section to this chapter in the accompanying workbook, you'll find an activity to help you identify some of the ways Jesus might be inviting you to follow him more closely. Read until you find something that challenges you, then write that down and continue until you have a list of about ten challenges (more on this later). The first thing you will come across in Matthew 5 is the Beatitudes, and believe me, those are challenging to everyone if you ponder them for more than about ten seconds. Blessed are the poor, the merciful, the persecuted? Those set fire to the social script! I'd encourage you to pay attention to what is going on inside of you—look for the presence or lack of peace. Those could be signs that you should think about that passage a little more and maybe do something with it. By the way, did you know that the word *beatitude* can be translated as either "happy" or "blessed"? I think Jesus was on to something!

Two areas that I find particularly challenging to allow the Gospel to transform are highlighted by the fifth beatitude: "Blessed are the merciful, for they shall be shown mercy" (Mt 5:7); and in the middle of the Lord's Prayer, "Forgive us our sins as we forgive those who trespass against us." Maybe I have a heightened sense of justice and feel extra hurt, or maybe I'm just bad at forgiving others. Either way, I know this is one way that I am challenged to grow in self-gift. I also know that it will improve my relationships, especially the close ones.

The Smallest Possible First Step

St. Ignatius of Loyola, one of the great contributors to our rich tradition of prayer and spirituality, recommends an approach for when someone is having difficulty accepting God's will. If you don't desire to do God's will for you, then he suggests praying for the desire to do God's will, assuming you can do that. If every fiber of your being is resisting the urge to be a gift to a friend, then perhaps you could pray for the desire to be a gift in that moment. Or perhaps you can take it a level deeper and say you want to pray for the desire for the desire, and so on.

In therapy, this is analogous to the incremental steps that we encourage people to take as a way of overcoming fear, building up empathy, or developing a variety of healthy emotional and psychological habits. What you are looking for is simply to take the smallest possible step in the right direction, yet one that still challenges you. When I suggested that you read through the gospels to find ten challenging teachings of Jesus, I had this step in mind. For each of those ten things, what is the smallest step you can take in the direction you think God might be calling you? Are you called to forgive? Maybe start by, for one week, praying for the desire to forgive. If you find that you have the desire sooner than that, great! After that, you can graduate to praying for the courage to forgive someone *in your mind only*. Then, if it is appropriate, you could eventually work up to forgiving them in person, verbally and explicitly.

You could also create a list of ten baby steps toward more selfless friendship and love in a variety of relationships. Why not try letting someone choose the restaurant or movie next time, doing a household chore that's usually not your responsibility, or giving an extra smile or hug? You can make it as easy as you would like. Just try to make sure it still challenges you a little bit, but not so much that you can't do it. Once you've created a list of ten items, choose the one that feels the easiest for you to accomplish. Start with the lowest hurdle, as you truly are seeking the easiest and smallest step to take toward self-giving love. After you've practiced that baby step for one week, you can then add a second step, and so on until you've built up to the tenth or, in your view, most challenging step.

If this seems too easy and not challenging enough, I encourage you to give yourself permission to do something easy. The temptation will be to tell yourself that something so small can't be worth anything. Please, trust me. I have seen tremendous growth in people who commit to taking baby steps in the right direction. But when people try to commit to something too big, I more frequently see them become intimidated with the challenge and never start.

As you begin taking baby steps, you can start to link them all together, like keeping a streak on social media. When you start building selflessness day after day, week after week, it accumulates into something truly amazing: you start to live as an icon of the Trinity and make the perfect love of Jesus visible in the world. This is how you avoid separation, division, and loneliness. This is how you discover deep emotional intimacy. This is how you live out your calling to authentic connection.

The amazing thing is that there is no ceiling for this trajectory. God places no limits on how much of his love and how much of his life we can experience. He can never run out! When we think we have gotten to the end, we find that there is only deeper and more satisfying love. It is a bond strong enough that even death cannot break it.

Who Is My Neighbor?

The next step is learning to identify who is your neighbor. Why? In God's wisdom, he has chosen for us to be interconnected with the people nearest to us. They are the ones with whom we must establish authentic connection and emotional intimacy if we are to experience God's love more fully. In the Gospel of Luke, we hear the parable of the good Samaritan, which challenges the cultural norms of the day. The scholar who asks Jesus "Who is my neighbor?" is like so many of us when we want to be cheap with our love and self-gift. He may have been looking for validation of loving those whom he found easy to love, but Jesus wanted more for him. This parable is about how members of someone's community were unwilling to break a cultural taboo to help and yet someone from a despised outsider group was willing to show great love to a stranger in need. Did you ever think about how Jesus makes the Samaritan the good guy? Isn't that great?

Like the scholar who approached Jesus, we may be tempted to limit the amount of love required in the Christian life by drawing a circle around people who are easy to love and excluding the ones who aren't. Perhaps we are afraid that we are unable to love and extend ourselves to that degree. But rather than put limits on our ability to love as God loves, why not ask how we can allow Jesus's teachings to further expand our capacity for love? Who are those people in our lives for whom we haven't romanticized the idea of love and self-gift? They are the people who need us most.

If you were to ask Jesus, "Who is my neighbor?" what would he say? He might respond by asking, "Who are the people you are responsible for?" Or maybe he might ask, "Who is already within your closest circles, those within arm's reach?" Sometimes in faith circles we have the impression that we need to love with grand gestures. We often overlook the people that God has placed directly in front of us, in our lives. If we are to be his hands and feet, why not start with what is happening right in front of us? The works of mercy can be fulfilled within the walls of your domestic church, your extended family, and your workplace. A parent can clothe and feed their naked and hungry children. Friends and roommates can bear wrongs patiently, forgive one another, and learn to live more like the good Samaritan and less like the scholar who wanted to justify himself.

Nora made a gift of herself to her children in this way. When she made the decision to live a chaste, single life and focus her energy on her children, everything changed. Her children were her neighbors, the ones she had to learn to love as herself. When she did this, her children really began to thrive. But it wasn't easy. It was a real sacrifice for Nora. Of course, she still desired a husband and was open to dating. However, she decided not to pursue dating at the expense of her children's needs. In doing so, she truly became a gift in her daily choice of love. For a guided activity on recognizing your neighbors, turn to the workbook pages for this chapter.

"I Just Don't Feel Like It Right Now"

Sometimes it's just plain hard to choose to love, and you may find that it is all too easy to ignore calls to self-gift. Parents don't always feel up to getting on the ground and playing with a young child. Adult children often feel too busy to spend time with an ill or aging parent or grandparent. We may avoid a friend who has fallen on hard times because we feel unsure of how to help.

Yes, these moments are hard, but I think that is a good thing for us. If we can train ourselves to recognize *when* we are resisting the call to self-gift, we can more easily grow in those areas when we find it challenging to develop deeper connections. Here are some steps you can take to learn how to recognize this disposition in yourself:

First, think back to the last time you knew you were being called to go outside of yourself and do something for someone. Was it responding to a call for connection from a friend, roommate, or spouse? Was it a child asking for your full attention when you were on the phone?

Consider the precise feeling you had at that time. Apathy? Ambivalence (wanting both to respond and to stay put)? Lethargy and exhaustion? This is an important step because we want this feeling to be a cue for a behavior that can help us overcome the inertia of doing nothing.

Now, you can add something like this to your list of baby steps: "The next time I feel this feeling, _____, I will respond by _____." Again, your immediate response doesn't have to be heroic; it can be the smallest possible step in the right direction.

If you don't like to give of your time to others, you could say, "The next time I feel myself dragging when my friend asks for help, I will immediately respond by generously offering more help than she asked for." If care for the poor doesn't come naturally to you, you could say, "The next time I feel irritated by a homeless person, I will respond by having a meaningful conversation with them, even if I don't offer them food or money." To grow in forgiveness, I might need to say something like, "The next time I feel angry or that I've suffered an injustice, I will immediately respond by praying for that person's goodness, happiness, and holiness, as well as by forgiving them in my heart."

Especially in a tense or heated dialogue, it's very easy to entrench ourselves and refuse to give up our position. When this happens in therapy sessions, I remind people about what is really at stake: the status of their relationship. If no one is willing to sacrifice their stance and make a gift of themselves, the issue between them will continue to block the path forward and is likely to cause them to drift further apart. It is usually at this point, once I describe the dynamic, that even the most stubborn person is willing to consider making a gift of themselves on behalf of the relationship. While your position will always feel important, your ability to give up that position in order to love the other person is key to preserving the health of your relationship.

When you have been legitimately wronged, and it will happen to all of us, it is difficult to let go of our anger or disappointment. In such situations, ask yourself, "Am I willing to forego all the joy, happiness, laughter, and love that this friendship will provide so that I can feel righteous for a little while?" While the angry side of you may say yes, I think you would agree that a more rational side of you would say no. If you haven't already done so, now would also be a good time to turn to the workbook and complete the accompanying activity and explore this more in depth.

Preserving Enough of Yourself to Give Away

When my father-in-law gave a eulogy at his mother's funeral, he started and ended with these words: "My mother is a unique and wonderful creation" (emphasis on *is*). In between these rhetorical bookends, he shared touching stories of what made his mother delightfully gifted. Without using these exact words, he spoke about how she revealed the goodness and glory of God in ways that only she could. He recognized that his mother was a gift to him and many others.

To love others deeply, we must first recognize that each of us is truly a gift. You too are a unique and wonderful creation who journeys forward in life in a way that no one else can emulate. You offer something that the people around you need yet no one else can give: yourself.

All our gifts, including our very selves, are meant for other people. Consider the voice of a great cantor, the creative genius of an artist, or the caring presence of an empathetic friend who has been there for you in life's most trying times. God gives us our gifts to give away for the good of others.

There is something about you that your community needs and can benefit from, something that only you can give. You were created for such a time as this (Est 4:14), and your friends and family benefit when you recognize that your presence is itself a gift. When you live this truth, it becomes easier to extend yourself as a gift to others.

But knowing that you have something to give and using those gifts are two different things. Ever heard the saying "You can't pour from an empty cup"? It's important to tune in to yourself from time to time and assess if you are thriving, especially in your gifted areas. If you find yourself low on energy or languishing cognitively, you may find it challenging to bring God's love to those around you.

In God's wisdom, he gave us the Sabbath, and he models the importance of rest. Consider this passage: "Seek first the kingdom [of God] and his righteousness, and all these things will be given you besides" (Mt 6:33). Rest is good, and we are made for it. When we seek it, we find that it will allow us to do so much more of what God has in store for us. If our priorities and self-care are aligned with God's plan for our lives, everything else will more easily fall into place.

What does self-care look like? Within moderation, it means that we recognize our basic human needs. When they were hungry on the Sabbath, Jesus broke the social script of his day and permitted his disciples to eat grain while walking through a field (Mt 12:1–8). Admittedly, it may be hard for us to take this seriously because we have such a different social script when it comes to keeping the Sabbath holy. But what if Jesus were to say that you should refuse to answer work emails on Sunday, or even after hours when you were spending time with family? Would you rationalize it and say that it is really okay, all the while recognizing the problem that it presented to your health and relationships? It is clear that Jesus ranks basic human needs, such as feeding and healing, as more important than things like social convention. That is because he cares about his creation and loves us. We are more important and have more dignity than mere convention.

Are you meeting your own basic human needs? Let's brainstorm for a minute and reflect on ways to engage in self-care. When I discuss self-care with others, I frequently come across the same topics. Sleep, healthy eating, exercise, and healthy friendships. These are what I consider to be baseline needs for living and giving ourselves away. Are you sleeping enough so that you can be joyfully present to others? Are you maintaining your health in a way that will allow you to make a self-gift to others for years to come? How are your eating habits? Do you get the chance to blow off steam through exercise and time with friends? Or are you aiming to satisfy the demands of a social script that does not respect your dignity, not now nor in the future?

There are other things to consider as well such as leisure, learning, or artistic enjoyment and expression. Are there talents that God has given you and that you would like to explore? Consider for a moment your friendships, your family, or the poor you could serve if only you had more energy or time. The 60, 70, or 90 year old you would be so grateful for the attentiveness you give yourself in your earlier years. Your family would be appreciative as well!

I do not say this with the intention to put more pressure or guilt on you. After all, we are talking about rest and rejuvenation. I ask these questions in order to help you reflect on ways you can integrate self-care into your regular life. Below are some examples of self-care, and you can find more examples in the corresponding workbook.

- Get sufficient quality sleep
- Regular exercise
- Invest time into quality friendships
- Actually use your lunch break at work
- Practice deep breathing—even as little as 90 seconds every 90 minutes
- Eat and/or prepare healthy, quality food that you love
- Deliberately expose yourself to nature
- Practice mindfulness while eating and drinking
- Do a body scan: close your eyes and think about your body head to toe, noticing any pain or tension and deliberately relaxing each body part
- Pray, even for as little as one minute
- Keep a gratitude journal—write one thing daily that you are grateful for
- Read something just for enjoyment
- Turn off your devices and enjoy the quiet
- Make time to watch the sunrise or sunset and enjoy the feeling of the sun on your skin

Now, self-care doesn't mean you live selfishly—that would be quite a thing for me to propose in a chapter about self-gift! Just as embodying the love of the Trinity is fulfilling because that is how we were designed, so too do we have a design that dictates how we thrive physically and emotionally. Self-care just means acknowledging that you have physical, mental, emotional, and spiritual needs that need to be met if you are to be fully alive. Please, for your own sake and for those around you, give yourself permission to take care of these needs.

Becoming an Icon of the Trinity

The dignity of being made in the image and likeness of God is that we make the mystery of God visible in our actions and interactions, how we live, and especially how we love. This is the why of everything, not just emotional intimacy and connection. This is the why of the Christian life, what we are called to do. It's why we follow Jesus and live as he lived. We make visible the sublime beauty of Jesus as members of his Body, the Church. When we make a gift of our lives to others as he did, we live the truth of who we are held in existence to be.

Throughout the history of Christianity, the Church has been referred to as the "sacrament of salvation" (CCC 776). What does that mean? Well, sacraments are things that make some invisible reality visible to humanity. They allow us to see God's actions, promises, and grace in a tangible way. They make it so that our senses can grasp divine activity, like in the water of Baptism, the bread and wine of the Eucharist, and the physical embrace of Marriage. But how is the Church a sacrament?

The earliest historical description of the Church is in Acts 2:42–47:

> They devoted themselves to the teaching of the apostles and to the communal life, to the breaking of the bread and to the prayers. Awe came upon everyone, and many wonders and signs were done through the apostles. All who believed were together and had all things in common; they would sell their property and

> possessions and divide them among all accord-
> ing to each one's need. Every day they devoted
> themselves to meeting together in the temple
> area and to breaking bread in their homes. They
> ate their meals with exultation and sincerity of
> heart, praising God and enjoying favor with all
> the people. And every day the Lord added to
> their number those who were being saved.

The Church—the people like you and me that Jesus gath-
ered together—makes salvation visible because we live the
truth that we have been set free to love one another as God
intended. The first Christians allowed the Gospel to transform their lives and change the social script so much that
they became an attractive curiosity to the outside world.
But it did something more than that. Jesus's transformative
love, his life coursing through our veins, allows us to live
as a sign to the world that we are made for more. A better
life is possible here, with even better things to come. We
become the tangible, sense-perceptible sign that the Passion, Death, and Resurrection of Jesus is real. It worked;
he lives, and we can live in him. That is how we are a sacrament of salvation.

When people see us thriving in our relationships, they
see the love of the Trinity, the mystery and meaning of life.
This happens to the degree we live according to God's
plan. When we live otherwise, we become anti-sacramen-
tal, incarnating something that is not true to who God is
and how he made us. These are the type of people who
wound others, cause loneliness, and who live a lonely life
themselves. But that is not your destiny; that is not what
you were made for.

I encourage you to journey bravely onward in the mystery of God's love. He wants you to know his love from
the inside, to know the joy of communion and authentic

connection. Please, continue to wade into conflict, dare to be vulnerable, seek healing when needed, and be the gift that only you can be. Loneliness, isolation, and separation cannot stand the light and truth of the life that God has planned for you. "I came so that they might have life and have it more abundantly" (Jn 10:10). Let's go!

Appendix

Questions to Add Detail to Your Relationship Road Map

See page 8 for more information about Relationship Road Maps.

Self

- Would you describe yourself more like a rushing stream or a slow-moving river? A mountain or a wave? A sunrise or a sunset?
- What is your favorite way of spending time with friends/with me?
- What is your favorite way of receiving and expressing love and affection?
- What do you wish everyone knew about you?
- When you retire or move away, what do you hope people say about you? What do you wish to be known for?
- What is one reputation you are afraid of?

God

- What is your preferred way of relating to God? As a child? A friend? A brother or sister? A lover?
- What is your favorite way to pray?
- What is your favorite feast or holy day?
- Who is your favorite saint?
- What is your favorite book of the Bible?
- What is your favorite scripture quote?

Food

- What is your favorite restaurant? Dinner? Dessert?
- What are your guilty pleasures?
- What is your favorite type of food to cook?
- If you could only eat one food for the rest of your life, what would it be?
- What is the best meal you have ever had?

Leisure, Recreation, and Fun

- What is your favorite movie?
- What is your favorite TV show?
- Who is your favorite author or writer?
- What is your favorite book?
- Do you know any poems by heart?
- Do you have a favorite painter, sculptor, or visual artist? Who?
- What is your favorite sculpture or painting? Why?
- Who is your favorite band or musical artist?
- What is your favorite song?
- Do you prefer the beach or mountains?
- Where do you want to go on vacation next?
- What was the first album you purchased or were given?
- What was the first concert you ever attended?

Learning

- If you could study and become proficient in anything, what would it be?
- What was your favorite subject in school?
- What was your least favorite subject in school?
- What is one language you would like to learn? Why?

Exercise

- What are your favorite and least favorite types of exercise?
- What physical challenges would you like to accomplish in life?
- What is one physical challenge you have no interest in attempting?

Chores

- What is one chore you hate doing?
- What is a chore you would love for me to do more often for you?
- What is something you like to do together or with other people?

Retirement

- How do you hope to spend the latter years of your life?
- What job would you be willing to do for the rest of your life?
- Would you want to stay close to family and friends when you retire or move somewhere new?

Children

- How many children would you like to have?
- Would you consider adoption and foster care?

- What experiences would you hope to provide for your children?
- What do you hope your children can avoid experiencing?

Childhood

- How did your family vacation when you were younger, if you vacationed at all?
- What was your favorite cartoon or TV show as a child?
- What was your favorite restaurant, dinner, and dessert?
- What did you dream of doing when you were older?
- What sports or hobbies were you interested in?
- Who was your favorite teacher and why?

For Married Couples: Romance and Sex

- What are your likes and dislikes during sex?
- How do you want your spouse to romance you throughout the day?
- What do you enjoy doing after sex?
- Who do you want to initiate sex?
- What do you find arousing that would surprise me?

Regina Boyd is a licensed mental health counselor and marriage and family therapist. She is the founder of Boyd Counseling Services and a contributor to the Hallow app.

She earned a bachelor's degree in psychology from the University of Central Florida and a master's degree in mental health counseling from Rollins College.

Boyd has presented extensively on the intersection of mental health and Catholicism for national organizations including the Catholic Campus Ministry Association, Given Institute, FemCatholic, and the Archdiocese of Philadelphia. Her work has been featured by Catholic Women in Business and FemCatholic, and on SiriusXM's The Catholic Channel.

Boyd lives with her family in Orlando, Florida, where she assists with parish and diocesan marriage formation.

www.reginaboyd.com
Facebook: ReginaBoydLMHC
Instagram: @boydcounselingservices
Podcast: Connecting Out Loud

FREE COMPANION VIDEOS
TO ACCOMPANY YOU THROUGH EACH CHAPTER

Scan here to access these videos or visit
avemariapress.com/private/page/leaving-loneliness-behind-resources.

GET THE COMPANION WORKBOOK!

Leaving Loneliness Behind: The Workbook is the essential companion for Regina Boyd's book *Leaving Loneliness Behind*.
It provides exercises, charts, lists, ideas, interactive questions, and journaling space to put into practice the skills you've learned from the main book. Scripture reflections guide you to explore ways that connection with others will help you live God's plan for your life.

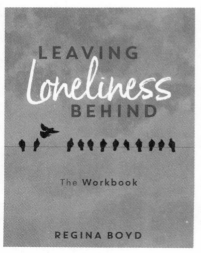

The workbook corresponds to each chapter of the main book and offers:

- a chapter summary;
- guided scripture reflections and prayer questions to deepen your relationship with God;
- a warm-up activity to prepare your mind and start identifying your goals;
- two main activities that break down your goals into doable steps by using charts, lists, diagrams, and reflection questions;
- a summary to pull together your goals, blind spots, and hopes into an actionable plan;
- practical tips as you begin working on your relationships in day-to-day life; and
- room to journal and chart your progress.